HYBRIDIZATION AMONG THE SUBSPECIES OF THE
PLETHODONTID SALAMANDER ENSATINA ESCHSCHOLTZI

WITHDRAWN

Ensatina eschscholtzi eschscholtzi × *klauberi*, hybrid.

HYBRIDIZATION AMONG THE SUBSPECIES OF THE PLETHODONTID SALAMANDER ENSATINA ESCHSCHOLTZI

BY
CHARLES W. BROWN

UNIVERSITY OF CALIFORNIA PRESS
BERKELEY · LOS ANGELES · LONDON
1974

UNIVERSITY OF CALIFORNIA PUBLICATIONS IN ZOOLOGY
ADVISORY EDITORS: G. A. BARTHOLOMEW, J. H. CONNELL, JOHN DAVIS, C. R. GOLDMAN, CADET HAND,
K. S. NORRIS, O. P. PEARSON, R. H. ROSENBLATT, GROVER STEPHENS

Volume 98

Approved for publication November 19, 1971
Issued December 14, 1974

UNIVERSITY OF CALIFORNIA PRESS
BERKELEY AND LOS ANGELES
CALIFORNIA

UNIVERSITY OF CALIFORNIA PRESS, LTD.
LONDON, ENGLAND

591.08
C153u
v. 98
1974

ISBN: 0-520-09442-5
LIBRARY OF CONGRESS CATALOG CARD NUMBER: 71-187743

© 1974 BY THE REGENTS OF THE UNIVERSITY OF CALIFORNIA
PRINTED IN THE UNITED STATES OF AMERICA

CONTENTS

Introduction	1
Acknowledgments	2
Account of the Subspecies	3
Review of the literature	3
Methods and Materials	6
Collecting	6
Color analysis	7
Areas of study	10
Descriptions of Parental Populations	12
Ensatina eschscholtzi xanthoptica	12
Ensatina eschscholtzi platensis	13
Ensatina eschscholtzi eschscholtzi	14
Ensatina eschscholtzi klauberi	14
Color Analysis	14
Sierra Nevada Populations	14
General aspects	14
Calaveras Big Trees region	16
Bass Lake region	23
Conclusion and summary	32
Southern California Populations	33
General aspects	33
San Gorgonio Mountain region	33
Palomar Mountain region	40
Miscellaneous Southern California regions	43
Conclusion and summary	44
Biochemical Analysis	46
Methods and materials	46
Variation in the subspecies	46
Analysis of the hybrid zones	47
Conclusions and summary	49
Discussion	53
Summary	55
Literature Cited	58
Plates	59

ERRATUM

University of California Publications in Zoology, Volume 98
Charles W. Brown: *Hybridization among the Subspecies of the
Plethodontid Salamander Ensatina Eschscholtzi*

On the verso of the title page:
Issued December 14, 1974 *should read* Issued September 14, 1974

HYBRIDIZATION AMONG THE SUBSPECIES OF THE PLETHODONTID SALAMANDER ENSATINA ESCHSCHOLTZI

BY

CHARLES W. BROWN

(A contribution of the Museum of Vertebrate Zoology, University of California, Berkeley)

INTRODUCTION

IN SOME SPECIES of animals a series of interbreeding populations are connected by intermediate forms, which in their geographic distribution form a loop, but which do not interbreed at the sympatric terminal portions of that loop. Such species provide examples of the initial stages of genetic divergence which may lead to speciation (Ehrlich and Holm, 1963). Mayr (1963) noted twenty species of animals in this category. Among them are the Herring Gull (*Larus argentatus*), the White-Footed Mouse (*Peromyscus maniculatus*), the Solitary Bee (*Hoplitis producta*), and the subject of this monograph, a plethodontid salamander, *Ensatina eschscholtzi*. In addition to those listed by Mayr, the Wandering Shrew (*Sorex vagrans*) was reported by Findley (1955) and the Red-eyed Towhee (*Pipilo*) by Sibley (1950).

Varying degrees of genetic divergence between the overlapping terminal forms are to be found among these examples. In *Pipilo*, for instance, genetic divergence between the Red-eyed and Collared Towhees is great enough to warrant their recognition as distinct species. In some areas reproductive isolation is complete, and the two species co-exist sympatrically without hybridizing, while in other areas some introgressive hybridization occurs (Sibley, 1950). However, there are numerous examples of polytypic species which are distributed roughly in a circle, but which have intermediate populations between all adjacent subspecies, even between those which diverge greatly. In Gilbert's skink (*Eumeces gilberti*), for example, genetic divergence has progressed to a point at which phenotypic differences are clearly evident, although apparently not enough divergence has occurred to achieve a major reduction in reproductive capacity even between the markedly differentiated subspecies.

Ensatina eschscholtzi is an intermediate example between the two above-mentioned species (Stebbins, 1949). Because of obvious geographic variation in its striking color patterns and its circular distribution (see fig. 1), it is an outstanding example of a Rassenkreis.[1] It is polytypic and its races are distributed in the

---

[1] The term "Rassenkreis" was first coined by Rensch (1929, 1960) as synonymous with polytypic species. Since then the term has been used in the sense of a circle of races in which there is overlap of the terminal portion without interbreeding. Mayr (1963) pointed out Rensch's original usage and noted the more recent usage, when applied only to cases of circular overlap, as incorrect. I feel that if Rassenkreis and polytypic species are regarded as synonymous, no useful purpose will be served, but in fact another burdensome term will be added. Therefore, I propose that the term Rassenkreis be changed from the original meaning as defined by Rensch to: *Rassenkreis*: a polytypic species in which there exists a chain of interbreeding populations distributed in a circular pattern, the terminal forms of which meet or overlap without interbreeding, or with only infrequent hybridization.

mountains of California in the form of a circle, kept open by the aridity of the Great Valley. The subspecies along the coast, with the exception of *picta*, are unblotched dorsally, whereas those in the more interior mountains are variously spotted or blotched. The two series of subspecies intergrade in the mountains of northern California. Over 400 miles to the south, their southernmost terminal populations are sympatric and appear to be almost completely reproductively isolated. In the foothills of the central Sierra unblotched populations, presumably derived from the coast, live in contact with blotched populations with which they interbreed. This study investigates the extent of genetic discontinuity between the unblotched and blotched forms, as well as the frequency of introgressive hybridization between them in areas where populations of the two types are in contact.

ACKNOWLEDGMENTS

Throughout the last fifteen years, I have had kind cooperation and assistance from many people, and I wish to express sincere thanks to all, especially those with whom I have worked closely recently.

First and foremost, I wish to express my deep appreciation to Professor Robert C. Stebbins, Museum of Vertebrate Zoology, University of California, Berkeley. His kindness and patience over these many years have enabled me to complete this work in spite of many difficulties.

In addition, some of my former students, Dr. Richard Chole, Mr. Robert Fine, Dr. Steve Allen, Jr., Mr. Charles Ault, and Mr. Paul Key have greatly assisted me in collecting specimens during the initial difficult years of learning the nature of activity periods and specific habitats of *Ensatina*.

Dr. Samuel McGinnis, California State College at Hayward, and Dr. Allen G. Brown, Fullerton Junior College, also made helpful suggestion and assisted me in collecting. Dr. Richard Etheridge, California State College at San Diego and Mr. Michael Long, California State College at Los Angeles provided valuable specimens which otherwise would have been most difficult to obtain.

I wish to thank Mr. Jack Mendenhall, the owner of extensive land near Palomar Observatory, for permission to collect on his property. The National Park Service and National Forest Service were helpful in granting permission to carry out parts of my study in some of the forests and parks of California. The ranger naturalists at Palomar State Park were helpful in providing local weather data and a temporary storage place for can traps to be used in other areas.

I wish to express special thank to Ms. Emily Reed, illustrator in the Department of Zoology, University of California, for the superb illustrations; to Mr. Al Blaker and the staff of the Scientific Photography Laboratory, University of California, for the high quality photographs and suggestions for illustration used in this thesis. Mr. Ken Owen, Business Manager, Zoology Department, University of California, helped in obtaining special funds for the long field trips throughout the state.

Thanks are due Dr. G. Ledyard Stebbins, University of California, Davis, and Dr. Allan Wilson, Biochemistry Department, University of California, Berkeley, for reading the manuscript and providing valuable suggestions and advice.

Finally, special thanks to Ms. Sue Gangwer for the many hours of typing and retyping of the manuscript.

ACCOUNT OF THE SUBSPECIES
REVIEW OF THE LITERATURE

In 1949 Stebbins published an intensive study of the geographic variation in *Ensatina* throughout its entire range. Prior to his analysis, four species were recognized: (1) *E. eschscholtzi* from the Pacific Coast Ranges from British Columbia to San Diego County, (2) *E. sierrae* from the Sierra Nevade of California, (3) *E. croceater* of Southern California from Fort Tejon of Kern County in the Tehachapi Mountains to the mountains of San Diego County, and (4) *E. platensis* known only from one specimen from Montevideo, Uruguay, and possibly others from Buenos Aires in Argentina.

In his intensive collecting, Stebbins found interconnecting populations between the coastal unblotched *E. eschscholtzi* and the interior blotched *E. sierrae* in the mountains of northern California. Intermediates between the blotched *E. croceater* and *E. sierrae* were found in the southern Sierra Nevada. Although there was a discontinuous distribution of the blotched *E. croceater*, the color patterns indicated a trend from a northern form near Fort Tejon, Kern County, to a southern form in San Diego County via the San Bernardino Mountains. Finally, the specimen, presumably from Uruguay, was determined to be essentially identical to *E. sierrae*, and because of its questionable locality, it was considered to be *E. sierrae*. The Argentina specimens were reexamined by Myers and Carvalho and were considered not of the genus *Ensatina*.

Because the four species of *Ensatina* were found to be connected by intermediate populations, Stebbins concluded that *Ensatina* was a single species. Seven subspecies were recognized: *E. e. picta, oregonensis, xanthoptica, eschscholtzi, platensis, croceater,* and *klauberi*. They are distributed throughout California, Washington, Oregon and British Columbia, as shown in figure 1. Recent minor range extensions have modified the map published by Stebbins (1949).

Stebbins (1949) found that the coastal unblotched subspecies *xanthoptica* also existed in a narrow range on the west slopes of the Sierra Nevada adjacent to, but at lower elevations, than *platensis*. At that time only a single individual, which was intermediate between the sierran *xanthoptica* and *platensis*, was collected on Jawbone Ridge in Tuolumne County. All other individuals collected at that locality seemed to be distinctly *xanthoptica* or *platensis*. All other Sierran *xanthoptica* analyzed by Stebbins were isolated specimens from various localities in the Sierran foothills. No other point of contact between blotched and unblotched populations was known in the Sierra Nevada.

In Southern California no intermediates had ever been found between the unblotched populations of *eschscholtzi* and any of the blotched forms. This suggested strongly that the blotched and unblotched populations were not interbreeding. Stebbins (1949) summarized the situation as follows:

Increasing genetical divergence is inferred from the progressive morphological divergence between the coastal and interior series of races to the south of their juncture in northern Califoraia where the mountain systems they inhabit are connected. In this area they are united by

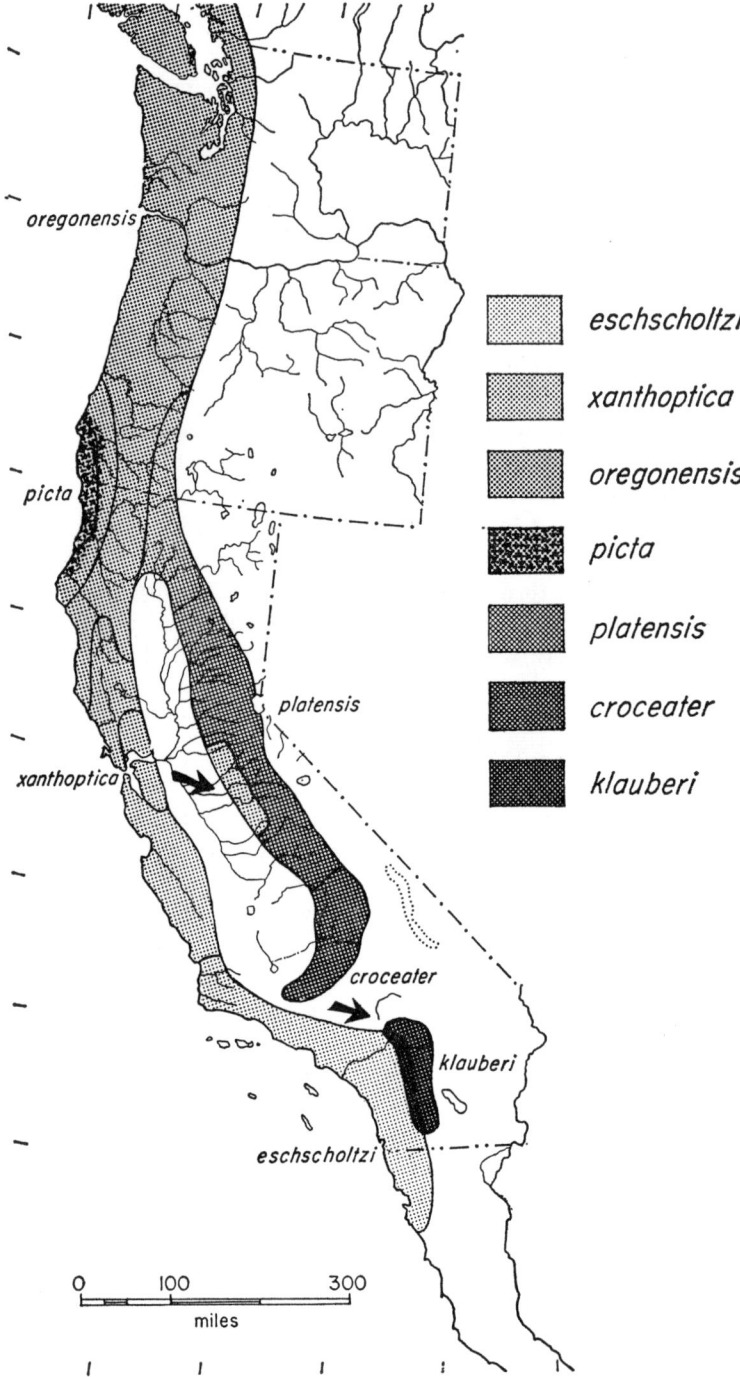

Fig. 1. Distribution of the subspecies of *Ensatina eschscholtzi*.

an extensive, smoothly intergrading population. This southward divergence is further borne out by the behavior of sympatric poplations to the south. From a zone of free interbreeding in the area of intergradation, one passes to a region where partial reproductive isolation seems to exist (Sierran populations of *xanthoptica* and *platensis*) to complete isolation commonly found at the species level as appears to exist between *eschscholtzi* and *klauberi* of southern California.

The obvious difficulty in this interpretation was the lack of conclusive evidence that the blotched and unbloched subspecies would not interbreed if sympatric populations existed. In fact no sympatry, in terms of cohabitation at precisely the same locality, had been observed and this was noted by Stebbins (1949) and commented upon by Dodson (1952). In addition, the populations of *xanthoptica* found to be in contact with *platensis* were limited to a single locality. Thus the evidence supporting Stebbins's concept of a Rassenkreis in *Ensatina* was in part negative and was, therefore, not a strong case if only geographic distribution was considered. However, the striking difference in color patterns between the unblotched form *eschscholtzi* and the blotched form *klauberi* motivated investigators to continue the search for zones of sympatry.

Stebbins (1949) reported an individual of the subspecies *eschscholtzi*, obtained at Harbison Canyon, four and one-half miles southwest of Alpine where Klauber had reported the blotched form *klauberi*. However, no additional specimens have ever been reported in the intervening area.

Stebbins (1957) turned his attention to another area of possible sympatry. In the San Bernardino Mountains, in the vicinity of San Gorgonio Mountain, *eschscholtzi* had been collected at Forest Home in Mill Creek Cayon. Dunn's (1929) paratypes of *klauberi* were labeled "Mill Cañon, Banning Water Cañon, Banning, Calif." Thinking the two localities were identical, Stebbins attempted to find *klauberi* in the Mill Creek area, but failed. He then turned to the headwaters of the White Water River, which also drains water from San Gorgonio Mountain but in an easterly direction. In this attempt he learned from the Banning Water Company that a small tributary of the San Gorgonio River, which drains in a southerly direction from San Gorgonio Mountain, is called Mill Canyon (Sawmill Canyon on United States Topographic Maps; see fig. 14) and should not be confused with Mill Creek which drains to the west. Furthermore, Stebbins learned that Arthur Gilman, the collector, was still alive and that he had found a "black and pale colored" salamander near a waterfall in a tributary at the headwaters of the San Gorgonio River above Banning. Intensive collecting in this tributary (Sawmill Canyon = Mill Canyon or "Water Canyon") by Stebbins in 1956 yielded both the blotched form, *croceater-klauberi* intergrades, and *eschscholtzi*. The two forms were found about 0.2 miles apart. None of the blotched or unblotched individuals seem to show any evidence of genetic introgression between the two populations. Although Stebbins conceded the possibility of interbreeding, he stated that Sawmill Canyon was "an area of seemingly unquestionable sympatry" (but not necessarily cohabitation).

The viewpoint that the two chains of *Ensatina* populations met in Southern California without interbreeding persisted in the literature for an additional twelve years (Mayr, 1963; Ehrlich and Holm, 1963). In 1959 I found *eschscoltzi* and *klauberi* within 0.2 mile of one another near Palomar Observatory, and this discovery supported Stebbins's viewpoint

However, Stebbins and I, in an intensive search of Sawmill Canyon (Brown and Stebbins, 1964), found a presumed hybrid between the blotched and unblotched forms as well as two apparent backcrosses. The discovery of these hybrids indicated that interbreeding was possible between the blotched and unblotched subspecies of *Ensatina*, but there remained several questions: (1) At what frequency does hybridization occur? (2) What is the extent of genetic introgression between the parental populations? and (3) If a low frequency of hybridization is present, what are the reproductive isolating mechanisms?

In the years since the discovery of the hybrid from Sawmill Canyon, I have intensively collected and analyzed color patterns and blood proteins to answer, if possible, the first two questions. The evidence indicates that there is in fact only a very limited amount of interbreeding and introgression between blotched and unblotched populations in Southern California, but the question of the nature of reproductive isolating mechanisms still remains unanswered. I have also investigated the extent of hybridization between blotched and unblotched populations in the Sierra.

METHODS AND MATERIALS
Collecting

Ensatina were collected in three basic ways: (1) on roads, (2) by searching the habitat, and (3) by using dead fall can traps.

During the first fall rains, there is a sharp increase in the activity of *Ensatina*, with the majority of individuals moving up the hillsides, presumably as a feeding response or to avoid flooding. After the temperature drops during late fall and winter, mass movement across the ground surfaces stops. However, if a relatively warm rain should occur, there is again a great deal of surface activity. During these warmer rains, collecting *Ensatina* is quite simple. In fact, individuals have been obtained in much larger numbers than would otherwise be collected by other methods. This is particularly true for *xanthoptica* in the Sierra Nevada and *eschscholtzi* in the coast ranges of Southern California. Usually the greatest number of specimens are observed on roads between sunset and midnight.

The unblotched form of *Ensatina* north of Big Sur and the blotched forms *platensis* and *klauberi*, are found in greatest abundance when the habitat is searched. No good method has been devised for collecting *eschscholtzi* or *croceater,* probably because *eschscholtzi* tends to be trogloditic and *croceater* is apparently rare. Most specimen collecting is done by turning logs or moving other forms of litter, such as boards and pieces of bark. Moving rocks has not yielded very many specimens.

In habitats marginal for *Ensatina*, in hybrid zones, and in other areas where it was essential to collect an adequate sample of a particular population or subspecies, the use of dead-fall can traps was particularly successful. From one can, for example, CSMA No. 3 near Bass Lake, a total of thirteen individuals were collected over a three-year period: six were *xanthoptica* and seven were *platensis*, and of these, several provided distinct evidence of genetic introgression between the parental populations. In two other cans, one at Fish Camp and the other at Westfall Campground, over a dozen individuals were collected in each at a single time. These traps were about 14 in. high and were made of two cans about 6 in. in diameter and 8 in. deep, telescoped together. In the bottom 1 in. of the can, a layer of soil was placed, topped by about 6 in. of excelsior. Holes were punched in the sides of the cans above the 1-in. level to allow excess water to escape. The soil and excelsior kept the cans damp—in some cases throughout the entire summer. The cans were sunk into the ground so that the tops were at ground level. Piles of loose bark, limbs and a few leaves were placed over the openings. It was necessary to avoid placing the bark too tightly down on the openings, or no individuals would fall into the can.

Most individuals collected were kept in captivity for a short time (2 to 8 weeks), and then the color patterns were analyzed. During this period of captivity, the salamanders were fed termites. Blood was removed from many individuals prior to preserving them, and the serum proteins were separated by acrylic gel disc electrophoresis. The details concerning these methods will be discussed in the section on biochemical analysis. After the blood was removed, the specimens were analyzed for color patterns and then preserved.

Color Analysis

In the color pattern analysis, the basic parameters used were abundance and distribution of melanophores, erythrophores, and iridophores over the entire body surface. A separation of melanophores and erythrophores produces the blotching found in *klauberi, croceater,* and *platensis*. A mixing of melanophores and erythrophores produces unblotched subspecies, such as *eschscholtzi, xanthoptica,* and *oregonensis*. Varying degrees of abundance of the various pigment cells are found in each population, and it is on these qualities of color patterns that many of the inferences concerning genetic divergence are based.

There are eight aspects of coloration used in this study: (1) blotching in the parotoid and head region (pl. 1); (2) blotching over the entire dorsal surface (pl. 1); (3) the degree of melanic development on the dorsal portion of the limbs (an average value of all four limbs) (fig. 2); (4) degree of iris iridophore development (fig. 2); (5) degree of erythrophore development on ventral surfaces (fig. 3); (6) degree of melanophore development on ventral surfaces (fig. 3); and (7) hue, value, and chroma of the color of the dorsal surfaces.

Stebbins (1949) found almost no iridophores in the eyes of *eschscholtzi* and *klauberi,* and therefore eye iridophores were not used in comparisons between blotched and unblotched forms of Southern California. No ventral erythrophores or xanthophores were observed in any unblotched form from Southern California, and in the blotched forms, *croceater* and *klauberi,* the only ventral erythrophores were ventral extensions of lateral blotches and were not considered in this study.

Using a combination of reference populations (representative of parental

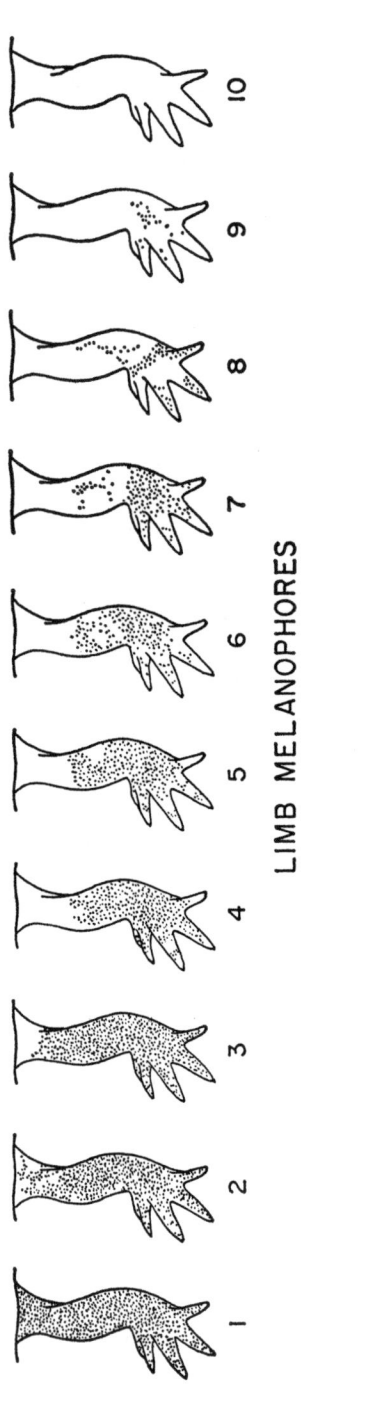
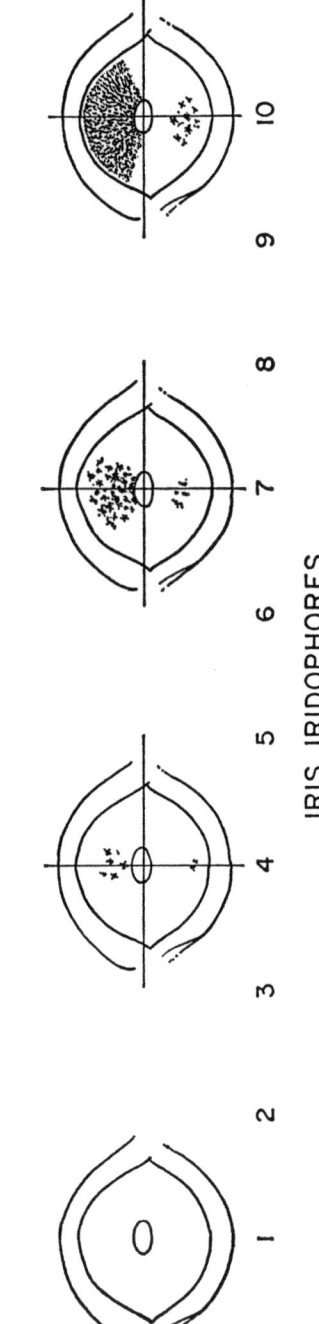

LIMB MELANOPHORES

IRIS IRIDOPHORES

Fig. 2. Standards used in studying limb and eye pigmentation in *Ensatina eschscholtzi*. Upper series: Range in degree of limb melanic development. Values of 2, 3 and 4, usually blotched forms. Values of 7, 8 and 9 usually unblotched forms. Lower series: Range in degree of iris iridophore pigmentation. Value of 1 = "pure" *platensis, croceater, klauberi,* and *eschscholtzi* populations. Value of 10 = "pure" *xanthoptica* populations. Intermediate values of 4, 5, 6 and 7 are most frequently found in zones of hybridization.

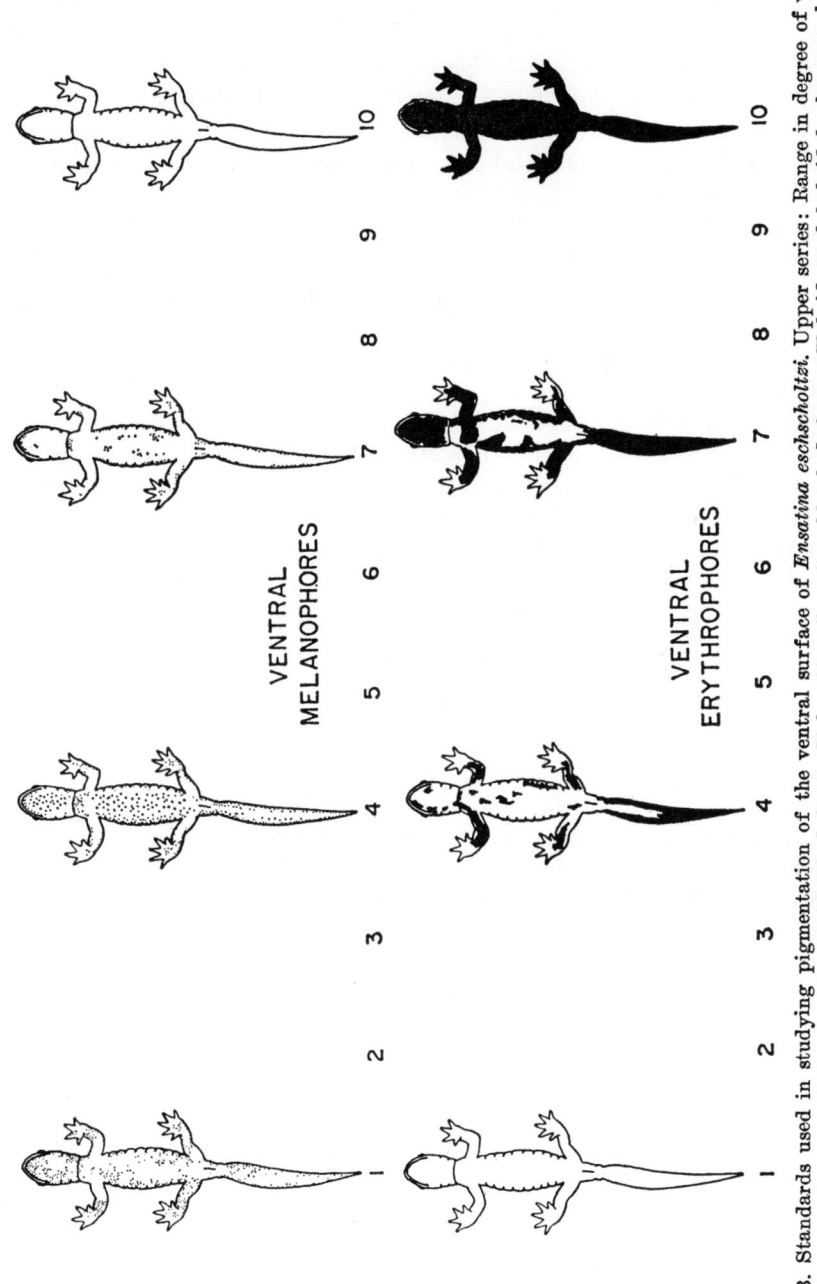

Fig. 3. Standards used in studying pigmentation of the ventral surface of *Ensatina eschscholtzi*. Upper series: Range in degree of ventral melanophore development. Value 1 = "pure" blotched forms. Value 10 = "pure" unblotched forms. Hybrids and hybrid backcrosses between blotched and unblotched forms have intermediate values. Lower series: Range in degree of ventral erythrophore development. Value 1 = "pure" *platensis, croceater, klauberi* and *eschscholtzi*. Value 10 = "pure" *xanthoptica*. Hybrid and hybrid backcrosses between *platensis* and *xanthoptica* have intermediate values.

stocks), described on p. 12 below, and hypothetical extremes, a scale of values was set up for the first six characters. Each character was assigned arbitrary values ranging from 1 to 10, with the number 1 representing a "pure" blotched form (*platensis, croceater,* or *klauberi*) and the number 10 representing a "pure" unblotched form (*xanthoptica* or *eschscholtzi*).

These values were then plotted on bar graphs as seen in figures 9, 12, 13, 18, and 19. The mean value for all characteristics of each individual was then plotted according to locality (figs. 8, 11, and 17). Both individual characters and mean values were treated in this way.

Intermediate values represent color patterns which were in some degree intermediate between the two "pure" forms and are presumed to be indicative of genetic introgression. Thus each individual, prior to preservation, was compared to the scale of values with respect to each of it six characteristics, and the value in each instance which most closely represented the individual being examined was recorded.

The analysis of the color quality of the dorsal surfaces of the salamanders was based on a comparison with chips in *The Munsell Book of Color*. (Color quality includes hue, value, and chroma, explained in the following paragraph.) Analysis took place under a standardized light resembling skylight (Macbeth Super Skylight Unit BX-848a). In the blotched subspecies, only the color of the blotches was considered, and this is produced almost entirely by the color of the erythrophores and xanthrophores. In the unblotched forms, however, the dorsal mixture of melanophores and erythrophores was evaluated. Because of this difference between these types of comparisons, values for blotched subspecies could not be fairly compared to values of unblotched forms. In figure 4, for example, the blotched form *platensis* can be compared with the blotched form *klauberi*, but not with *eschscholtzi*.

Color quality in the Munsell Book is expressed by three numerical values: (1) hue, (2) value, and (3) chroma. Hue refers to the place on the spectrum, that is, the wavelength being reflected from the surface. Value is the degree of intensity of light or dark. Chroma is the intensity of the particular pigment involved.

Hue, value, and chroma of the dorsal surfaces were analyzed separately and a coresponding numerical value was recorded for each individual.

After color analysis, the specimens were preserved and placed in the collection of the Museum of Vertebrate Zoology, University of California, Berkeley.

AREAS OF STUDY

The blotched and unblotched populations were found to meet in four localities (1) near Avery and Hunter Reservoir in Calaveras County (Calaveras Big Trees Region), (2) Lewis Fork Creek and Chepo Saddle in Madera County (Bass Lake Region), (3) Sawmill Canyon near Banning in San Bernardino County (San Gorgonio Mountain Region), and (4) Cedar Creek and near Dyche Valley in San Diego County (Palomar Mountain Region).

These four regions were chosen as areas of concentration of study, and are shown on the map in figure 5.

Brown: Hybridization of the Plethodontid Salamander   11

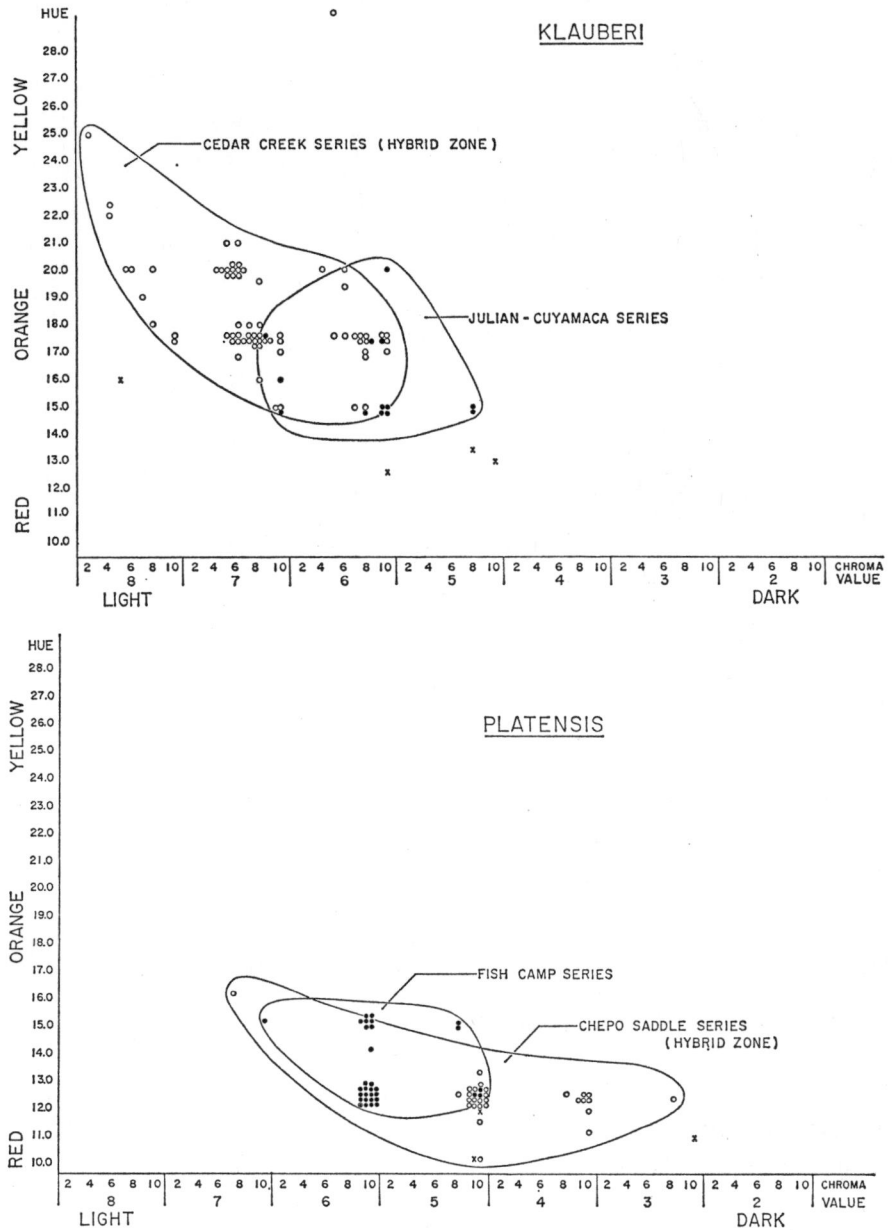

Fig. 4. Graphical representation of variation in hue, value, and chroma of the blotches of *Ensatina eschscholtzi platensis* and *E. e. klauberi*. Solid dots are values for individuals from localities relatively free from genetic introgression from unblotched populations. Open circles are values for individuals from hybrid zones. Note increased variability and shift in values for individuals of populations from hybrid zones as compared with those blotched populations not in contact with unblotched populations.

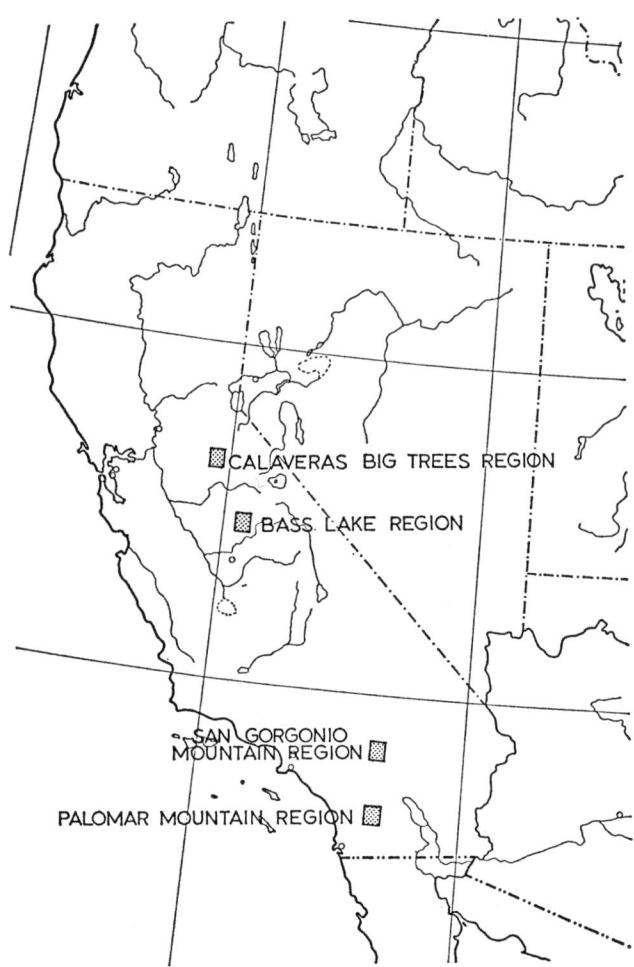

Fig. 5. Location of the four regions of intensive study upon which this paper is based.

DESCRIPTIONS OF PARENTAL POPULATIONS

In order to estimate the amount of introgression that has occurred between blotched and unblotched subspecies in their zones of overlap, the characteristics of typical representations of the parental populations must be described. Descriptions and localities of occurrence of these populations follow (see table 1 for numerical values):

Ensatina eschscholtzi xanthoptica.—Indian Creek headwaters, 3.0 miles west of Avery, Calaveras County, California.

Color quality: There is fairly uniform mixing of melanophores and erythrophores over the dorsal surfaces. Numerical values are: (1) hue 10.0 to 17.5—dark red to red orange; (2) value 2 to 6—near dark reddish brown to a light red; and (3) chroma—a almost black or gray to a deep heavy red, or red orange.

TABLE 1
Mean Values for Parental Populations of *Ensatina eschscholtzi*

	Elev. (ft.)	P	D	L	Eye L	Eye R	R	M	Ave	Hue	V	C
xanthoptica Indian Creek	3377		9.1	8.1	9.0	9.0	9.5	9.4	9.0	11.9	3.3	4.3
platensis Arnold	4069		2.3	5.5	2.1	2.3	1.2	3.4	2.8	12.4	5.5	9.9
eschscholtzi Southern California	4945	8.5	9.7	6.1	–	–	–	9.0	8.5	13.2	3.8	4.0
klauberi Julian and Cuyamaca State Park	4306	1.4	1.1	4.5	–	–	–	2.9	2.5	16.0	5.6	8.6

Dorsal pattern: Most individuals have a very slight degree of melanic concentration, usually on the dorsal surface of the head. A value of 10 represents a completely uniform mixing of melanophores. The mean value at Indian Creek is 9.

Eye iridophores: Iridophores of the eyes (forming a silver or gold eye patch) are abundant—9.0 in both left and right eyes. There is a very slight degree of asymmetry.

Ventral coloration: Ventral surfaces are almost entirely free of melanophores. Only a very few were observed on the ventral surface of the lower jaw in some specimens, giving a mean value of 9.4 for the population. There is heavy development of erythrophores both dorsally and ventrally. The ventral surfaces are usually covered solidly with red chromatophores and only a very few specimens have a small spot lacking these pigment cells. The mean value is 9.5. In general, the *xanthoptica* of the Sierra Nevada have a much weaker overall melanophore development than either *plantensis* or coastal *xanthoptica*.

Ensatina eschscholtzi platensis.—0.5 mile E.N.E. Arnold, 4100 feet, Calaveras County, California.

Dorsal pattern: There is a high degree of variability in dorsal blotching, but less so in populations more removed from hybrid zones. At Arnold there is a fairly distinct separation of the melanophores and erythrophores that produce the blotching effect, and melanophores are rare within the blotches.

Blotches are relatively small, having a mean value of 2.35. Numerical values for color quality of the blotches are: (1) hue, 11.5 to 15.0—more red than the reference *klauberi* population; (2) value, 4 to 6; and (3) chroma, 8 to 10. These figures are not comparable to *xanthoptica* values because in the analysis of coloration the blotches of *platensis*, which are relatively free of melanophores, were used. In *xanthoptica* there is a mixing of melanophores and erythrophores. However, as shown in figure 4, hue, value and chroma values are comparable among *platensis* and *klauberi* populations.

Eye iridophores: Highly variable. More asymmetry than in *xanthoptica*. Most individuals have values below 4.

Ventral coloration: Moderate to heavy development of melanophores. Values range from 2 to 4. Distribution relatively uniform. Ventral red chromatophores scarce. Only four out of the nineteen individuals analyzed had a very small blotch of erythrophores on the ventral surface. These blotches are usually not more than 2 mm in diameter, and often only one of them can be found.

Ensatina eschscholtzi eschscholtzi.—No good reference population could be collected for this study, and so a conglomerate of all individuals analyzed from zones outside of sympatry are used here as a rough base for comparison.

Dorsal pattern: Generally, the melanophores and erythrophores are fairly evenly mixed on the dorsal surfaces. However, in a significant number of individuals, there are some melanic concentrations, especially in the head and parotoid region.

Numerical values for color quality are: (1) hue, 10.0 to 17.5; (2) value, 2, 3, and 4 (with some paler individuals with values of 6 and 8); (3) chroma, of the latter, around 3, 4, and 5. The net effect in these pale animals is a "ghostly" pinkish brown.

Eye iridophores: None has been observed.

Ventral coloration: Ventral melanophores nearly absent. A few individuals possess a small scattering of melanophores on the interior ventral margin of the lower jaw but rarely elsewhere. No ventral erythrophores have been observed.

Ensatina eschscholtzi klauberi.—Mountains around Julian and Cuyamaca State Park, San Diego County, California.

Dorsal pattern: There is a relatively low degree of variability in dorsal coloration. Values for dorsal blotching range from 1 to 2 with a mean of 1.5. See Stebbins (1949: fig. 4) for information on the configuration for these blotches. Many individuals have the parotoid blotches connected across the head.

Numerical values for color quality of the dorsal blotches are as follows: (1) hue, 15.0 to 20.0; (2) value, 5 to 7; and (3) chroma, 8 to 10. The color of *klauberi* blotches tends to be more orange than in *platensis*.

Eye iridophores: Not analyzed. Presumed to be absent or extremely rare. Erythrophores absent, except at sides where color of blotches may encroach onto the ventral surfaces.

Ventral melanic development moderately variable with values ranging from 1 to 6, mean 2.9.

COLOR ANALYSIS
SIERRA NEVADA POPULATIONS
GENERAL ASPECTS

The blotched race, *Ensatina eschscholtzi plantensis,* occurs chiefly west of the Sierran crest, mostly above the 3600 foot elevation, from Lassen National Park southward throughout the forested region of the Sierra Nevada to the Greenhorn Mountains where it intergrades with the race *croceater*.

The major trees found at elevations above 5000 feet are Incense Cedar (*Libocedrus decurrens*), Sugar Pine (*Pinus lambertiana*), Lodgepole Pine (*P. murrayana*), Jeffrey Pine (*P. jeffrey*), White Fir (*Abies concolor*), and Red Fir (*A. magnifica*). At elevations between 3600 feet (hybrid zones) and 5000 feet are found (in addition to Incense Cedar, Ponderosa Pine, and White Fir) Live Oak

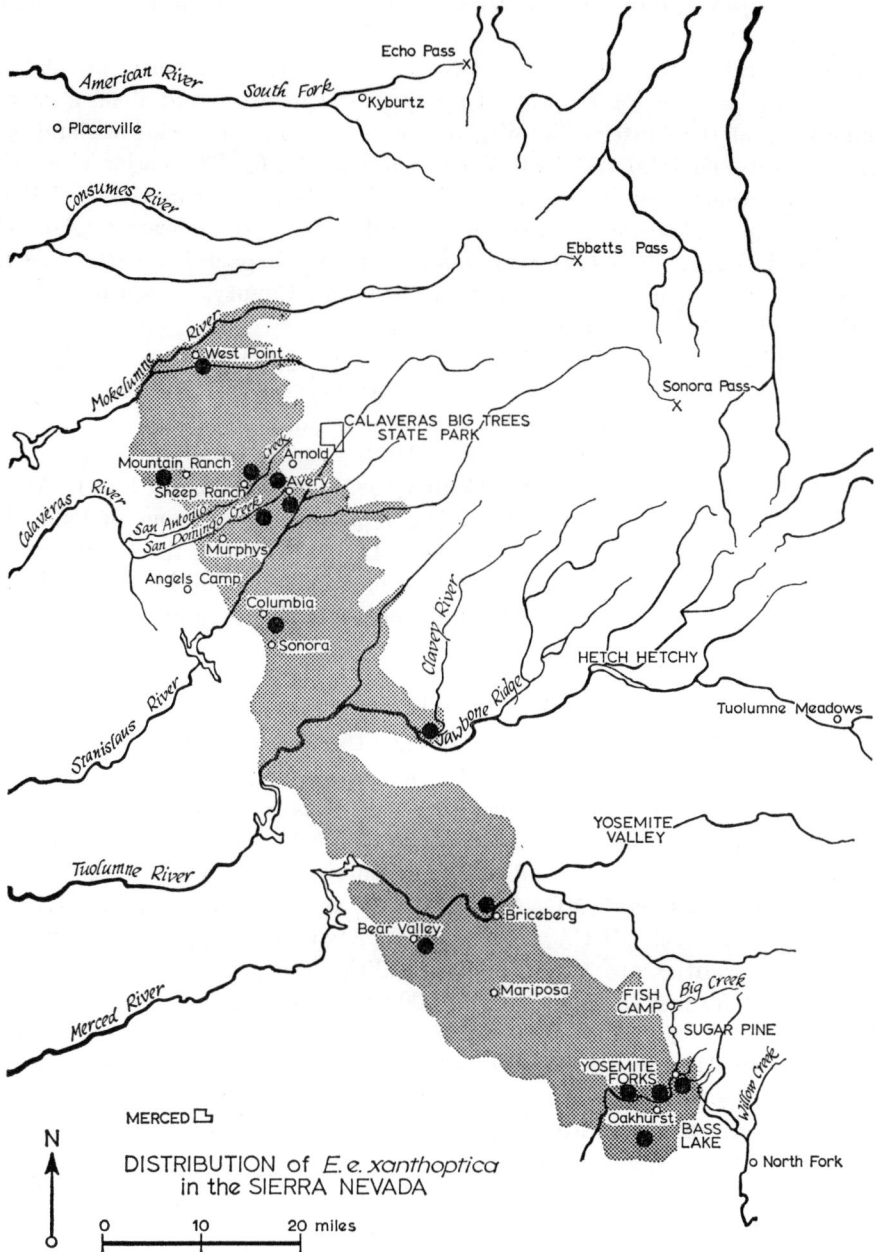

Fig. 6. Map of the distribution of known populations of *Ensatina eschscholtzi xanthoptica* in the Sierra Nevada. Stippled portion of map represents probable range based on knowledge of elevation, vegetation, and distribution of some *platensis* populations.

(*Quercus agrifolia*), Canyon Oak (*Quercus chrysolepis*) and Black Oak (*Quercus kelloggii*).

In the central portions of the Sierra Nevada there are a number of populations of the unblotched race *xanthoptica*. These populations are found along a narrow 95-mile strip of the western foothills, in regions of pine-oak, oak-grassland, and chaparral, between 1900 and 4000 foot elevations (fig. 6). The major vegetation at these elevations includes Ponderosa Pine, Live Oak, Canyon Oak and Black Oak in the Pine-Oak association. In the lower elevations are Manzanita (*Arctostaphylos*) and Digger Pine (*Pinus sabiniana*) in the chaparral. *Xanthoptica* has not been found north of West Point in Calaveras County, or south of Chepo Saddle near Bass Lake in Madera County.

The populations of unblotched *xanthoptica* meet populations of the blotched race *platensis* along the eastern limits for *xanthoptica* between 3000 and 4000 feet. However, where *xanthoptica* has not been found, *platensis* is found at lower elevations, such as 7.7 mi. E. junction of Dinkey Creek and Balch Camp Road, Kings River Camp No. 5, Fresno County, 885 feet (Stebbins, 1954). At the points where the two races meet, there is a relatively narrow zone of hybridization. Three such localities have been found. In two of these, the Calaveras Big Trees region and the Bass Lake region, the color patterns and blood protein distributions have been analyzed. The Calaveras Big Trees region in Calaveras County will be discussed first.

CALAVERAS BIG TREES REGION

General description of the study area.—The Calaveras Big Trees region, as defined in this study, is located about 120 miles east and 40 miles north of San Francisco in the central Sierra Nevada (fig. 5). This region is approximately 15 miles wide and 15 miles long and includes the following major localities at which *Ensatina* populations were studied: (1) Dorrington (DOCA), (2) Arnold (ARCA), (3) Mill Creek (MCAA), (4) Avery and Hunter Reservoir (HRCA) and (5) Indian Creek (ICCA). The letters CA stand for Calaveras County, in which these localities are found. These localities range from Mountain Ranch (MRCA) at 1950 feet to Dorrington at 5000 feet (see fig. 7).

The major stream drainages include San Antonio Creek, which drains to the southwest from Dorrington past Arnold and joins Indian Creek and eventually empties into the Calaveras River to the west. From Avery, San Domingo Creek drains to the southwest eventually joining the Calaveras River. From Calaveras Big Trees State Park, Love and Moran creeks flow southward and join to form Mill Creek near Avery. Mill Creek flows through Hunter Reservoir and then flows southward to meet the Stanislaus River.

Below 3000 feet, most of the San Antonio Creek, San Domingo Creek, and the Stanislaus River flow through deep canyons. Above 3000 feet, most stream drainages are gentle sloping ones and flow through pine-oak or cedar-pine forests. So in general, this region is characterized topographically by gentle rolling forested hills cut occasionally by deep canyons.

This region has a rather moist climate for California and a short dry season. The rains usually start in late October and end in early May, with occasional

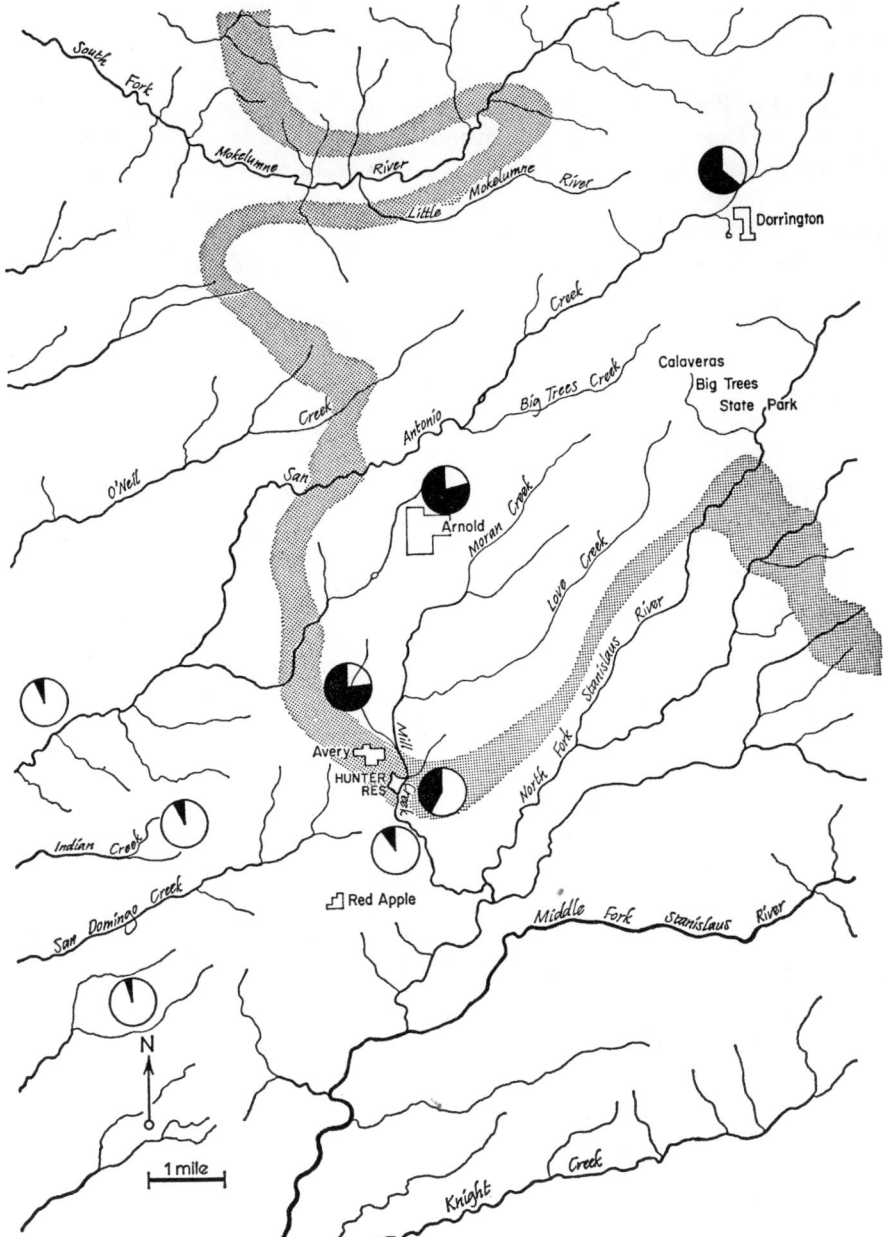

Fig. 7. Color variation in populations of *Ensatina eschscholtzi* in Calaveras Big Trees region in the Sierra Nevada. Stippled area represents possible hybrid zone. Pie diagrams are mean values for all six characteristics of the entire population for that locality, and expressed in percentages of 360°. An open circle would represent a hypothetical "pure" *xanthoptica* population completely free of genetic influence from *platensis* populations. A solid circle would represent a hypothetical "pure" *platensis* population completely free of genetic influence from *xanthoptica* populations.

summer thunderstorms in August and September. The warmth and moisture favor the growth of heavy coniferous and hardwood forests above 3000 feet. The forests above this elevation are fairly continuous and dense except for scattered open meadows. Below 3000 feet, depending upon local topography, the oaks and pines thin to some extent and the ground surface is only lightly covered with leaf litter, brush, and some exposed rock outcroppings. In the deep canyons, the situation is quite variable ranging from heavy oak cover to large areas of exposed rocky surfaces on the steep slopes.

Throughout this area, *platensis* has been found above 3000 feet, and *xanthoptica* from 3900 feet down to the 1900 foot level.

Color analysis and habitat descriptions (Fig. 7).—

1. Dorrington series (DOCA): This is the highest elevation in this region from which *Ensatina* was taken for this study. A total of eight *platensis* were collected from an east-facing slope about one mile north of Dorrington. Since the sample size is small, it is difficult to interpret the results of the color analysis. It seems as though there is a rather significant *xanthoptica* genetic influence on this population as two individuals were fairly heavily blotched, three possessed eye patches which were large relative to other *platensis* populations, and one had a small blotch of erythrophores on the ventral surface. However, it is clear that a much larger number of specimens needs to be collected around Dorrington to determine the phenotypic variation in the population (see figs. 8 and 9).

2. Arnold series (ARCA). Around Arnold, just south of Calaveras Big Trees State Park, is a heavy cover of Incense Cedar, Ponderosa Pine, and a few scattered Black Oaks. The leaf litter is deep, and there are many fallen logs at various stages of deterioration. Logging has occurred there, and some cabins are present in the locality studied, which is about one mile north of Arnold.

This *platensis* population has a relatively high degree of melanophore development and small blotches for the race. Values for dorsal blotching were quite low, generally 2, and only one individual had a value of 4. Fully half of the 38 eyes studied lacked iridophores entirely, and only 7 had values between 4 and 7. Five individuals had a very small spot of ventral erythrophores. The relatively heavy development of eye iridophores and the presence of ventral erythrophores are interpreted here as indications of genetic influence from *xanthoptica* populations. The ancestral *picta* stock probably possessed a very low incidence of eye iridophores.

3. Mill Creek series (MCCA): About six miles south of Arnold and 0.8 miles north of Avery, is a locality along the banks of a small tributary of Mill Creek. The gentle slopes around this stream are covered by heavy stands of Incense Cedar and Ponderosa Pine. To the south, the Incense Cedar thins out giving way to a thinner stand of pine and oak, which surrounds an extensive meadow just north of Hunter Reservoir and east of Avery.

At this locality, 0.8 miles north of Avery, 27 *platensis* were studied and found to have mean values from 2.0 (lowest for *platensis*) to 4.4. The range of values is the same as those in the Arnold population; however, more individuals show the influence of *xanthroptica* here. The following evidence indicates this greater *xanthoptica* influence: (1) five out of the twenty-seven individuals studied were

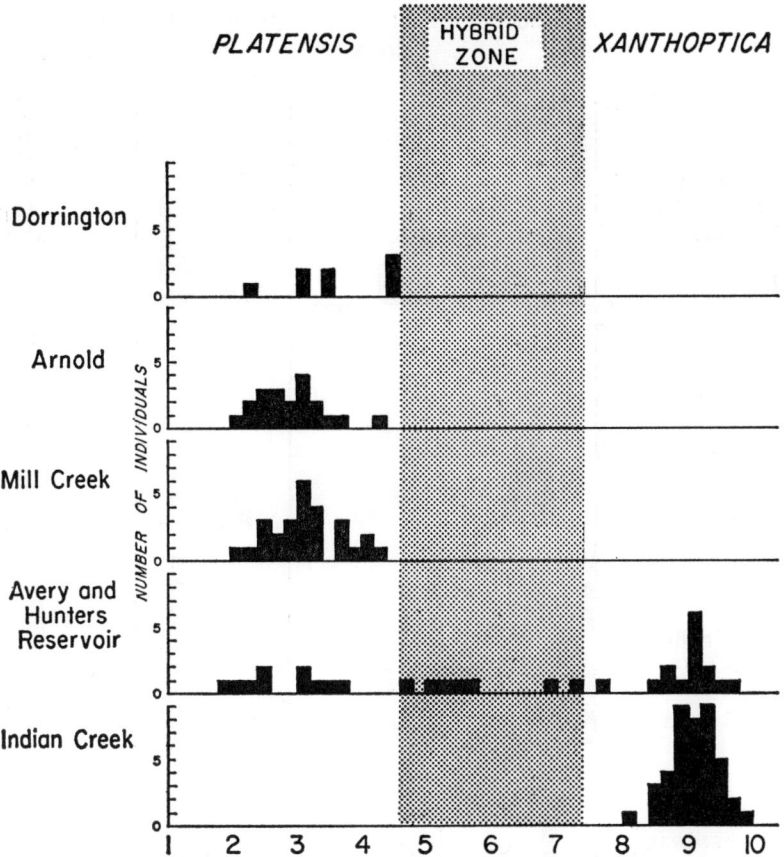

Fig. 8. Color variation is individuals of *Ensatina eshscholtzi* in Calaveras Big Trees region in the Sierra Nevada. Horizontal axis: mean value for each individual for six characteristics (dorsal blotching, limb melanophores, iris iridophores of right eye, iris iridophores of left eye, ventral melanophores, and ventral erythrophores). Vertical axis: number of individuals for each series.

heavily blotched, having values of 4 and 5; (2) the curve for limb melanophores is shifted to the right of the one seen at Arnold; (3) there is a high incidence of eye iridophores; (4) and there is a slightly lower development of ventral melanophores than those seen at Arnold. However, the occurrence of ventral erythrophores remains very low.

4. Avery and Hunter Reservoir series (HRCA): Just south and adjacent to the locality of the Mill Creek series is an expansive open area around Avery. This open meadow is surrounded by stands of Ponderosa Pine and Black Oak, except on north and east-facing slopes around Hunter Reservoir, which have a dense stand of Incense Cedar. To the south of Hunter Reservoir, the vegetation changes abruptly to an oak-chaparral association. To the east of Hunter Reservoir and east of Avery are open stands of pine and oak, which become more dense in stream drainages. The pine-oak association gradually gives way to oak-chaparral associations in San Domingo Creek drainage to the southwest.

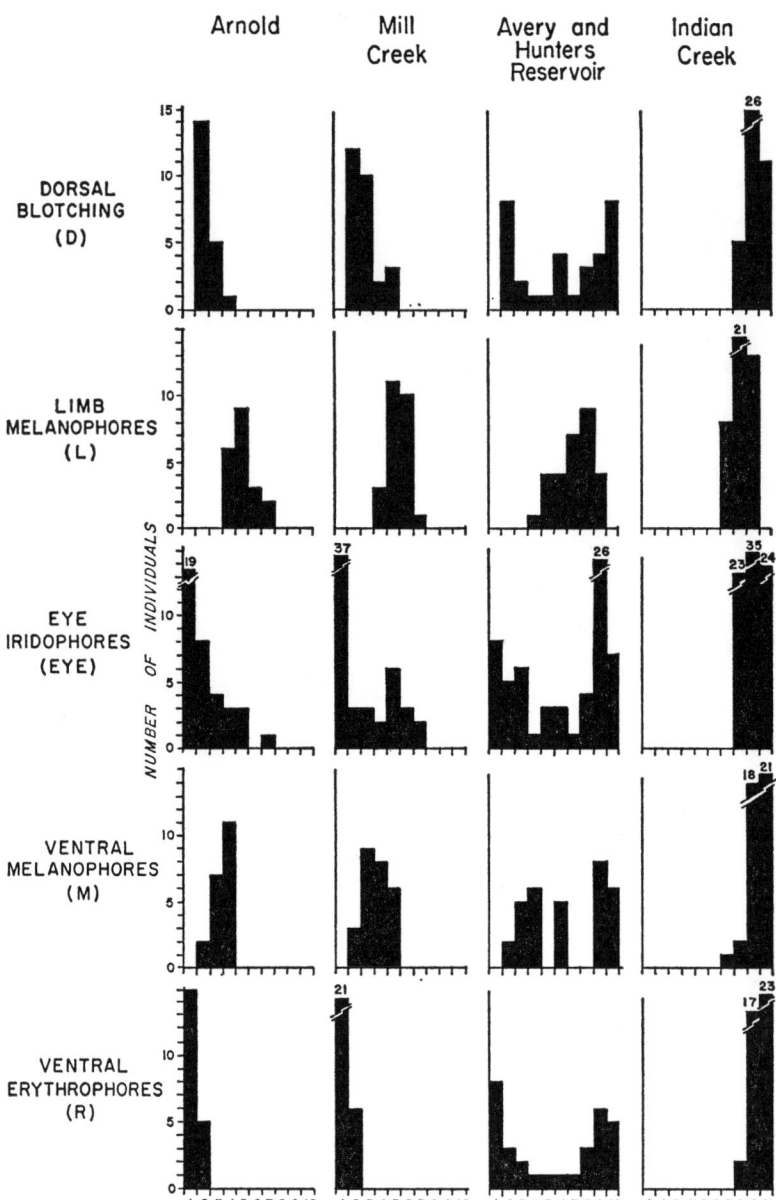

Fig. 9. Color variation in individuals of *Ensatina eschscholtzi* in Calaveras Big Trees region in Sierra Nevada. Horizontal axis: value of each characteristic for each individual. Left and right eye iridophore development values included in same graphs. Vertical axis: number of individuals for each series.

In this variable habitat, *xanthroptica* populations are found adjacent to and overlapping with *platensis populations*. In this series, seven intermediate individuals with values between 4.7 and 7.2 were found. For this reason, a strip of this area about one mile wide running northwest and southeast is considered a hybrid zone.

The distribution of the means of the five color characteristics analyzed demonstrates the bimodality of some of the values within this population. Dorsal blotching, eye iridophores, and ventral erythrophores are definitely bimodal in this area. There is some degree of overlap of distinctly blotched *platensis* (mean values of less than 3) with unblotched *xanthoptica* (mean values of more than 9) on the east side of Hunter Reservoir. The zone of overlap is estimated to be about 0.3 miles; however, more intensive collecting in the area will probably show that the overlap region is wider than observed here so far.

It is important to note in figure 9 at Avery and Hunter Reservoir the relatively high incidence of intermediate (5 and 6) values in dorsal blotching, eye iridophores, and ventral melanophores, as compared to values of 2 and 3 or 7 and 8. Perhaps this reflects a selection against backcrosses of hybrids with parental populations.

5. Indian Creek series (ICCA): Moving west from Avery along the ridge separating the San Antonio and San Domingo drainages, one finds a medium cover of pine and oak. About 2.5 miles west of Avery at the origin of the Indian Creek drainage is found a large population of *xanthoptica*. These specimens were easily collected by using dead fall can traps and by night driving in warm fall and winter rains.

In this *xanthoptica* population, the numerical values for all five characteristics were consistently high. Very few irregularities were noted in the dorsal coloration, that is there was a fairly uniform mixing of erythrophores and melanophores. In general, the melanophore development was very low in comparison with *platensis*, being almost entirely absent on the ventral surfaces. The entire surface both dorsal and ventral of most specimens was covered with a network of erythrophores. The effect of this pigmentation is a strikingly bright orange coloration, highly conspicuous to the human observer. This will be discussed in a later section on the adaptive value of color pattern in *Ensatina* races. The eye patches consisting of iridophores were found to be consistently large, most having values of 8 or higher.

6. Miscellaneous: Two individuals were collected at Sheep Ranch (2200 feet), and two more were obtained near Mountain Ranch (1950 and 2550 feet). These specimens had mean values of 9 or higher and the value of all characteristics fell within the normal range of *xanthoptica*. The lowest elevation at which *xanthoptica* was collected in this region is 2.6 miles southwest of Mountain Ranch. This locality is situated along the North Fork of Willow Creek and is covered primarily by chaparral except in the creek bottom where Live Oak cover predominates. This specimen (CWB 1134) was collected at night, while I was driving on the road from San Andreas to Mountain Ranch during a warm rain in February. I have found that this technique is best for collecting *xanthoptica* in the Sierra Nevada foothills. This subspecies is notoriously difficult to locate in the Sierra by

rolling logs, especially at the lower elevations of its range, which is also true of the *eschscholtzi* populations of Southern California.

Geographic correlation of colors.—

Dorsal blotching: In the populations of *platensis* at Arnold, there is a separation of dorsal erythrophores and melanophores[2] forming relatively small and fewer blotches than in populations at lower elevations. In the *platensis* populations at Dorrington, Mill Creek, and Hunter Reservoir, the blotches become larger and show greater degrees of irregularity (fig. 9). These irregularities include melanophores scattered throughout the blotches and highly irregular edges. In hybrids found around Avery and Hunter Reservoir, these irregularities are extensive, the melanophores forming reticulated networks throughout a background of erythrophores and varying sizes of melanophore patches. Of 129 individuals in the Calaveras Big Trees Region, only 9 demonstrated this highly irregular mixing of dorsal melanophores and erythrophores, with values of 5 and 6 on the dorsal blotching scale. The numbers of individuals which fell into each value were as follows:

Value	Number
2	38
3	18
4	5
5	5
6	4
7	1
8	8
9	30
10	19

The value "1" represents a complete absence of dorsal melanic blotching and no individuals were found in this hypothetical category, although some individuals were very close to this condition.

West of Avery, including Indian Creek, Sheep Ranch, and Mountain Ranch localities, the population was entirely of *xanthoptica* with most dorsal blotching values at 8, 9, and 10. Very little *platensis* influence could be observed at these localities, as the melanophores and erythrophores were fairly uniformly mixed. The few specimens collected southwest of Avery near Red Apple exhibit values around 9 also.

Ventral erythrophores: There is very little ventral erythrophore development in *platensis*. Out of 38 *platensis* with a dorsal blotching value of 4 or less, only 8 had one or two patches of erythrophores on the ventral surface and these patches were less than 2 mm in diameter. *Xanthoptica* is usually characterized by heavy ventral erythrophore development with values of 8, 9, and 10. In the hybrid zone around Avery and Hunter Reservoir, there is a distinct bimodality in the distribution and development of ventral erythrophores.

Iris iridophores: *Platensis* above 4000 feet have a considerable degree of variation in the development of iris iridophores. There is a direct correlation between

---

[2] There may be erythrophores scattered throughout the melanin covered portions but masked by this dark pigment. If so, they were not observed in this study.

the degree of variability and proximity of a *platensis* population to the hybrid zones. For example there are more individuals with iris iridophore values around 4, 5, and 6 in the Mill Creek population than in the Arnold population. In the hybrid zone there is a bimodal curve in the distribution and abundance of iris iridophores; however, bimodality is not nearly as distinct as in ventral erythrophores. In *xanthoptica*, the eye patches are usually large with values of 8, 9, and 10. *Platensis* have eye patches of values less than 7, except for one at Dorrington, which had a value of 8, and a dorsal blotch value of 2.

Ventral melanophores: Ventral melanophores exhibit very little bimodality in the populations of *Ensatina* studied in the Calaveras Big Trees region. There is little variability in Arnold, Mill Creek, and Indian Creek populations, whereas in Dorrington and Hunter Reservoir populations there is a much greater range of values. It is not clear why some of the individuals at Dorrington have such high values. A broad range of values is expected, however, in the hybrid zone near Avery and Hunter Reservoir. There is a striking absence of melanophores on the ventral surfaces of *xanthoptica* at Indian Creek.

Limb melanophores: There seems to be a fair amount of variability in the degree of melanophore development in *platensis* and in populations in the hybrid zones. Sierran *xanthoptica* have a general reduction in melanophores. The limbs therefore possess few of these pigment cells, and as a possible result of introgression, there is an increase in this melanic development in individuals from hybrid zones. There is a low correlation between limb melanophore values and dorsal blotching values.

BASS LAKE REGION

General description of the study area.—The Bass Lake Region, as defined for the purpose of this study, is an area situated about 150 miles east of San Francisco and 50 miles north of Fresno, in the western foothills of the central Sierra Nevada (fig. 5). This region is approximately 20 miles long and 10 miles wide and includes the following major localities from which specimens of *Ensatina* were obtained: (1) Kelty Meadow (KMMA); (2) Fish Camp (FCMA); (3) Sugar Pine (SPMA); (4) Lewis Fork Creek (LFMA); (5) Yosemite Forks (YFMA); and (6) Chepo Saddle (CSMA). The letters MA stand for Madera and Mariposa counties in which these localities are found. These localities range from Miami Creek (MCMA) at 2000 feet to Kelty Meadow at 6400 feet (see fig. 10).

There are three major stream drainage systems in this region, all eventually draining to the west. In the northern portion of the study area, is the west-draining Big Creek and its tributaries. Part of its upper drainage flows through Kelty Meadows. This system first drains west then turns north through Yosemite National Park, eventually reaching the Merced River.

The second drainage system is the Lewis Fork, Nelder Creek, and Redwood Creek, which are tributaries of the Fresno River. Lewis Fork and Nelder Creek flow south and meet Redwood Creek before flowing into the Fresno River.

The third drainage system include the north fork of Willow Creek, which drains south from Kelty Meadow, through Bass Lake and eventually into the San Joaquin River.

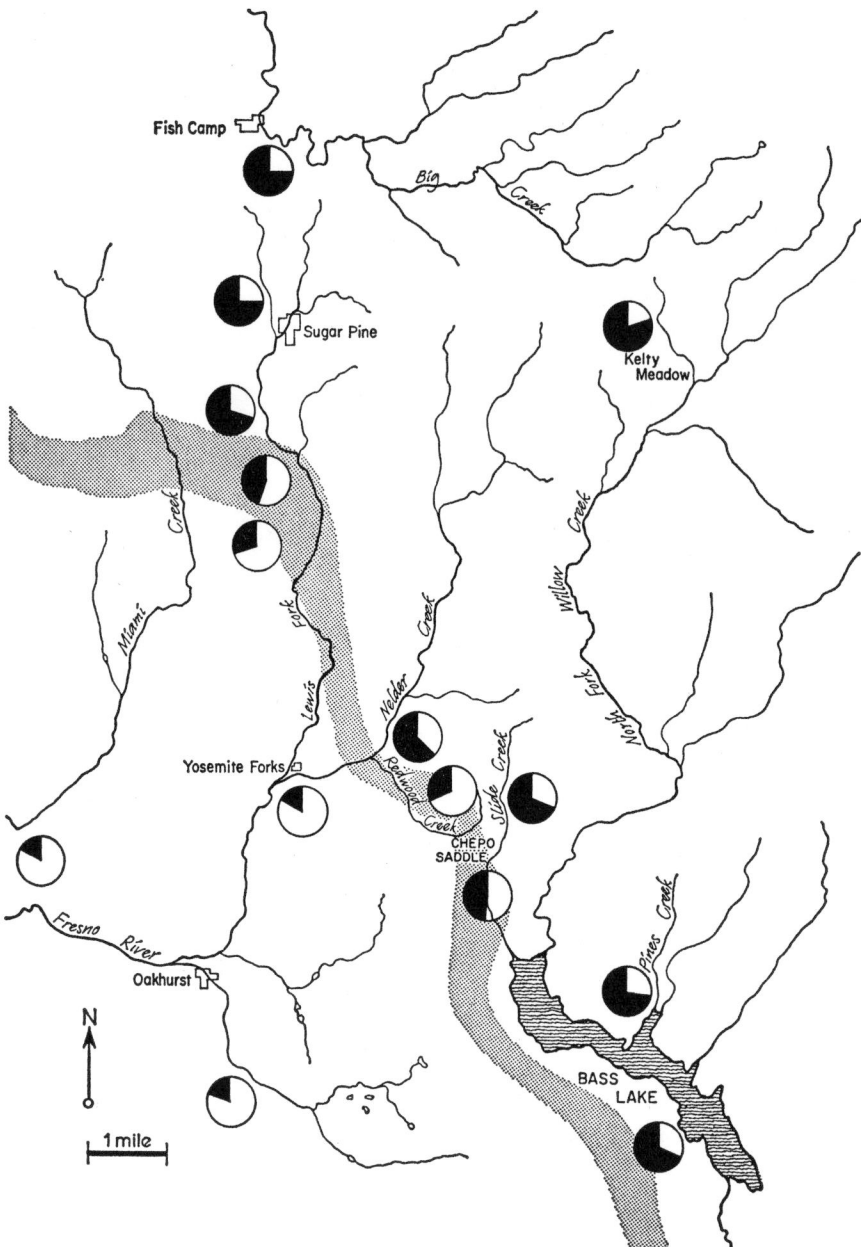

Fig. 10. Color variations in populations of *Ensatina eschscholtzi* in the Bass Lake region in the Sierra Nevada. Stippled area represents possible hybrid zone. Pie diagrams are mean values for all six characteristics of the entire population for that locality, and expressed in percentages of 360°. An open circle would represent a hypothetical "pure" *xanthoptica* population completely free of genetic influence from *platensis* populations. A solid circle would represent a hypothetical "pure" *platensis* population completely free of genetic influence from *xanthoptica* populations.

In general, much of the topography of this region is characterized by gentle hills and mountains, which are not particularly steep or cut by deep river gorges. The streams move through moderately wide and gently sloping drainages which are covered by heavy vegetation, logs, and leaf litter above 3000 feet. At lower elevations, the vegetation is more sparse, leaf litter thin or nonexistent, and rock outcropping more evident.

For most of the Bass Lake Region, the vegetation is favored by a fairly moist climate with a short dry season, June through September. The snow level quite often occurs between 3500 and 4500 feet which, interestingly enough, is the general elevation of contact between *xanthoptica* and *platensis* populations.

The vegetation in the Big Creek drainage is highly variable. In higher elevations along this drainage, there are numerous meadows, exposed rock outcroppings, and occasional heavily forested hillsides. The forest becomes more dense near Fish Camp and then changes to chaparral below.

To the south of Big Creek along the Lewis Fork and Nelder creek drainage, the Ponderosa Pine and Incense Cedar forests are heavy down to the 3600 foot level. At that elevation, the cedar populations thin out and are replaced by oak and chaparral. The change at 3600 feet is rather abrupt in many places, and this coincides roughly with the hybrid zone between *xanthoptica* and *platensis*. Below Yosemite Forks at 2800 feet, oak and chaparral are predominate, but there are some scattered Digger Pine.

The Willow Creek drainage is similar—at about 3600 feet, depending on the local topography, cedar-pine associations are replaced by pine-oak; then around the 2800 foot level, pine-oak is replaced by oak-chaparral-grassland type vegetation.

In general, *platensis* populations are found above 3200 feet in the cedar-pine association when *xanthoptica* is found below 3900 feet. However, when *xanthoptica* is not present, *platensis* has been found as low as 2400 feet, for example in the Willow Creek drainage at North Fork.

Color analysis and habitat descriptions.—

1. Kelty Meadows Series (KMMA): In the higher elevations (6000 feet), at the upper drainage system of Big Creek and Willow Creek, there is a heavily forested locality. This area, between Kelty and Kramer meadows, is about two miles long and ranges between 5750 and 6400 feet in elevation. The dense coniferous forest is located on a southwest facing slope and includes Incense Cedar, Sugar Pine, Lodgepole Pine, Jeffrey Pine, White Fir, and Red Fir. Leaf litter is about 6 to 18 inches deep, and rotting logs are abundant. The slopes around the streams are gently sloping in most places.

About 25 can traps were positioned at this locality and a total of 6 individuals were obtained here. These specimens have about the same degree of variability in their color patterns as those found as Arnold, 50 miles to the north, and fall within the range typical for the subspecies *platensis* (see figs 8 and 11).

2. Fish Camp Series (FCMA): At about 5000 feet on the south side of Fish Camp, there is a heavily forested north-facing hillside covered mainly by Incense Cedar, White Fir, and Jeffrey Pine. To the north of the ridge above this slope is the Big Creek drainage and to the south is the Lewis Fork Creek drainage.

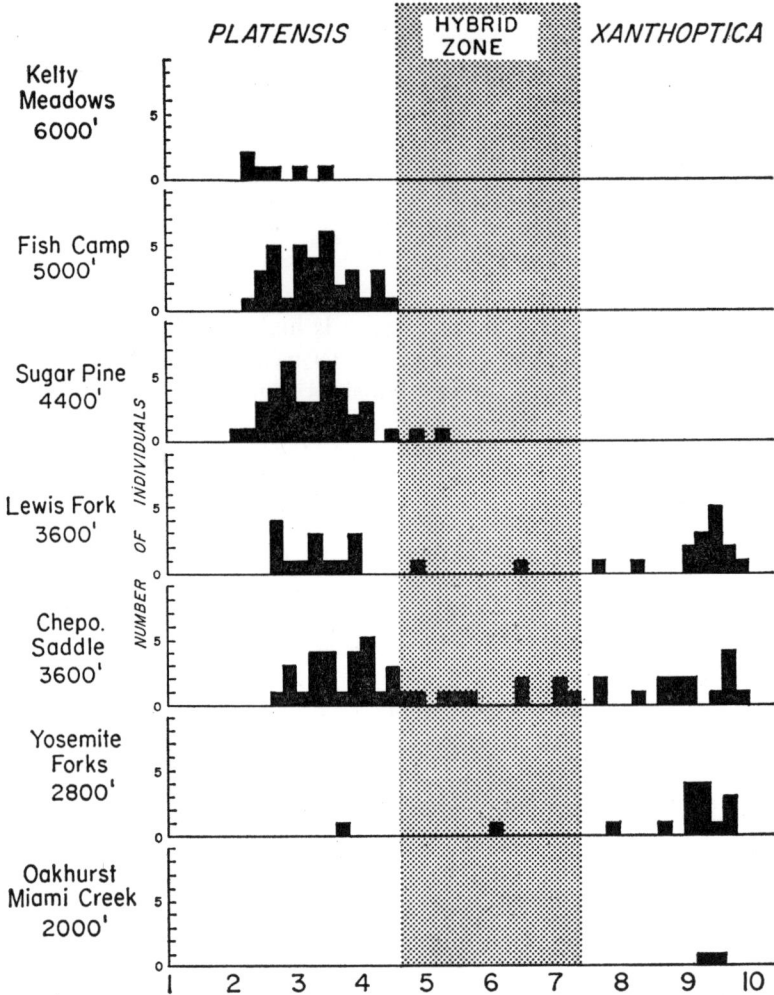

Fig. 11. Color variations in individuals of *Ensatina eschscholtzi* in Bass Lake region in the Sierra Nevada. Horizontal axis: mean value for each individual for six characteristics (dorsal blotching, limb melanophores, iris iridophores of right eye, iris iridophores of left eye, ventral melanophores, and ventral erythrophores). Vertical axis: number of individuals for each series.

Climatic conditions on the north slopes of this ridge differ markedly from the south-facing slopes, with temperatures as much as 15° cooler on the north-facing slopes, according to the National Forest Service records.

Thirty-five individuals were collected and analyzed from this slope. Again the color pattern falls within the normal range for *platensis*, the highest mean value of the average characteristics being 4.4. There is, however, a rather high incidence of eye iridophores among a number of individuals. To the north and downstream about 2 miles along Big Creek, is a rather open area covered by chaparral and scattered pine, indicating greater aridity. Perhaps *xanthoptica* occurs nearby, possibly to the east or north. This might be the basis for apparent *xanthoptica* influence, as demonstrated by the eye iridophores.

3. Sugar Pine Series (SPMA): South from Fish Camp and downstream along Lewis Fork Creek lies Westfall Campground and Sugar Pine at about a 4300 to 4500 foot elevation. Westfall Campground has a very heavy cover of Incense Cedar, Ponderosa Pine and White Fir. Around Sugar Pine about one mile southeast of Westfall, the coniferous forest cover is more sparse, with large open areas evident.

Color patterns of the 39 individuals analyzed show a somewhat greater range in variation than at Fish Camp. Two individuals showed enough *xanthoptica* genetic influence to be considered in the "hybrid" range. There is a considerable degree of eye iridophore development in the population and dorsal blotching; however, the other characteristics fall within the normal range of *platensis*.

4. Lewis Fork Creek Series (3600 feet) (LFMA): At a locality 1.6 miles south of Sugar Pine, the vegetation changes rather abruptly from a heavy cedar-pine to a pine-oak-chaparral association. In the cedar-pine association, the leaf litter is deep (6 to 18 inches), and the tree cover more dense. In the more arid pine-oak-chaparal association below 4000 feet, leaf litter is thinner and there are more rock outcroppings than seen above 4000 feet near Sugar Pine. It is at this locality that the blotched *platensis* populations meet the unblotched *xanthoptica* populations.

Analysis of color patterns of individuals in the Lewis Fork Creek area, at around a 3600 foot elevation, demonstrates that it is a hybrid zone. The patterns closely resemble those which exist in Chepo Saddle and Avery populations. There is a definite bimodality in the degree of development of dorsal blotching, ventral erythrophores, and ventral melanophores. There exists a greater range of values, but not a bimodal distribution, in the degree of limb melanophore development, compared to the Fish Camp series.

Blotched and unblotched individuals with little evidence of introgression have been collected at various locations between 3000 and 4000 foot elevations, indicating that there is sympatry with infrequent interbreeding. For example, in the Lewis Fork drainage, nine *xanthoptica* with mean values of 9.3 and above have been found at 3500 feet and higher, and seven *platensis* with values below 3.3 have been collected below 3500 feet.

5. Yosemite Forks Series (YFMA): The area around Yosemite Forks is characterized by scattered oaks, occasional pines, open grassy areas and considerable rock outcropping. This locality is at the junction of Lewis Fork and Redwood Creek, which after joining then drop rapidly south of the town of Yosemite Forks, in a rather deep canyon. Upstream in Redwood Creek the oaks become more abundant and within half a mile one finds a heavy mixture of pine and oak with a large open meadow at the junction of Nelder and Redwood creeks, about one mile east of Yosemite Forks.

Xanthoptica populations are predominant here, but only three individuals show evidence of extensive introgression with *platensis*. One *platensis* individual was located at the junction of Redwood and Nelder creeks. A juvenile hybrid was found just half a mile downstream from this point. Most of the *xanthoptica* were collected about 0.1 mile south of Yosemite Forks at a locality characterized by steep slopes and massive rock outcroppings. These *xanthoptica* were collected on Highway 41 during a drive in the rain at night.

South of Yosemite Forks, one *xanthoptica* was found 1.5 miles south of Oakhurst (2800 feet) and another at the junction of Miami Creek and Fresno River (2040 feet). Neither individual showed any indication of introgression with *platensis*.

6. Chepo Saddle Series (CSMA): The largest collections of individuals in a hybrid zone were obtained within a one mile radius of Chepo Saddle. *Xanthoptica* were found along Redwood Creek and along the east facing slopes of the Slide Creek drainage south of Chepo Saddle. North and east of this narrow zone, *platensis* were found in large numbers. Totals of 27 *platensis*, 15 *xanthoptica* and 9 hybrids were collected in this area.

To the northwest of Chepo Saddle is the Redwood Creek drainage. This drainage is covered by moderate to heavy stands of pine and some Incense Cedar on the north facing slopes of Redwood Creek. On the ridge to the west, the oak and pine thin out considerably and are replaced by some chaparral and grassy areas.

To the east of Chepo Saddle there is a heavy stand of pine and cedar in Slide Creek. South of Chepo Saddle there are open stands of pine and oak as well as a broad open meadow, which ends at Bass Lake about 1.5 miles south of the ridge.

The greatest degree of introgression between *xanthoptica* and *platensis* is evident in this series. There is a distinct bimodal curve of mean values shown by the graph in figure 11 and the range of *platensis* and *xanthoptica* values are shifted to the center. There is a biomodality in dorsal blotching, eye iridophores and ventral erythrophores which is similar to the Avery and Lewis Fork series. Again the range of values for limb melanophores and ventral melanophores is greater in this hybrid zone than in areas away from the zone of contact between *xanthoptica* and *platensis*.

7. Miscellaneous: The entire length of Willow Creek, from Kelty Meadows (6000 feet) around Bass Lake (3300 feet) down to the town of North Fork (2700 feet), four miles south of Bass Lake, is populated by *platensis*. No *xanthoptica* have been found here, even below the 4000 foot level. Therefore it is thought that the ridge separating the Fresno River and Willow Creek drainages may be the southern limit of distribution for *xanthoptica*.

Geographic correlation of characters.—

Dorsal blotching: Similar to the Calaveras Big Trees region, the most obvious patterns which clearly demonstrate a discontinuity between adjacent *xanthoptica* and *platensis* populations is the extent of dorsal blotching (figs. 12 and 13). In *platensis* populations such as those found at Kelty Meadows, Fish Camp and Sugar Pine, there is usually a separation of the melanophores and erythrophores forming blotches of varying numbers and sizes. In the elevations above 5000 feet the size and number of blotches are usually smaller than those below this elevation. Below 5000 feet the amount of erythrophore development increases both on the dorsal surfaces and on the limbs. In the hybrid zone (3000 feet to 4000 feet) there exists a distinct bimodal curve in the distribution and abundance of these two chromatophores. Usually specimens collected between 3000 and 4000 feet are either distinctly blotched, with melanophores and erythrophores separated (*platensis*), or the two types of pigment cells are relatively mixed in a uniform manner (*xanthoptica*). However, the hybrids show varying degrees of irregularity, which is to say there is irregular mixing of melanophores and erythrophores. The blotches when present in "*platensis*-like hybrids" have highly irregular edges and melanophores are scattered within the blotches, sometimes as irregular networks. These hybrid patterns are uncommon. Out of 83 individuals, only 8 clearly had this mixing effect, the remainder demonstrated only very slight mixing (*platensis*) or a uniform mixing (*xanthoptica*).

Ventral erythrophores: Most *platensis* above 4000 feet lack ventral erythrophores entirely. The few exceptions found at Fish Camp and Sugar Pine have only a single small blotch of erythrophores on the ventral surface, and this blotching is less than 2 mm in diameter. *Xanthoptica* found at elevations below 3000 feet (Yosemite Forks, Miami Creek and Oakhurst) usually have a uniform and complete network of erythrophores over the ventral surfaces. There are in some individuals a few small portions of the ventral surface which lack pigment cells entirely.

In the hybrid zones along Lewis Fork Creek and near Chepo Saddle, there is a striking bimodality in the distribution and development of ventral erythrophores. Only a few intermediates have been observed. These intermediates (possibly F_1 hybrids) have incomplete development of ventral erythrophores. The illustration in figure 3 shows these intermediate conditions. Often in these "presumed" hybrids, the irregular patches which lack erythrophores contain irregular scattered patches of melanophores. However, there seems to be no correlation between the distribution of erythrophores and melanophores when the two are found together in hybrids. This means that there is no specific blotching pattern formed as seen on the dorsal surface of *platensis*.

Iris iridophores: *Platensis* shows considerable variability in the development of iris iridophores. Most individuals above 4000 feet at Fish Camp, Kramer Meadow, and Sugar Pine lack the eye patch entirely. Of the *platensis* which possess this character, most individuals have a slightly unequal development between the two eyes, and the numerical values lie between 1 and 7. The left and right eyes are usually very close in the degree of iridophore development; however, one individual possessed no eye patch in the right eye and a large one in the left eye with a value of 7. The range of variability is greater at Sugar Pine than Fish Camp. None were found in the specimens from Kramer Meadow. In the hybrid zones, at Lewis Fork Creek and Chepo Saddle (around 3600 feet), there is a bimodal curve in values, but not nearly so clear as seen in dorsal blotching and ventral erythrophores. Most individuals possess values of 1, 4, 5, 9, or 10. Values of 2, 3, 6, 7, and 8 are much less frequent. *Xanthoptica* found at Yosemite Forks, Oakhurst, and Miami Creek have large eye patches, most with values of 9 or 10 (refer to figs. 2, 12, and 13).

Ventral melanophores: In contrast to ventral erythrophores, the degree of melanophores development on the ventral surfaces is highly variable in both *platensis* and *xanthoptica*. *Platensis* at Kramer Meadow, Fish Camp, and Sugar Pine generally have fewer melanophores than the population at Arnold, but con-

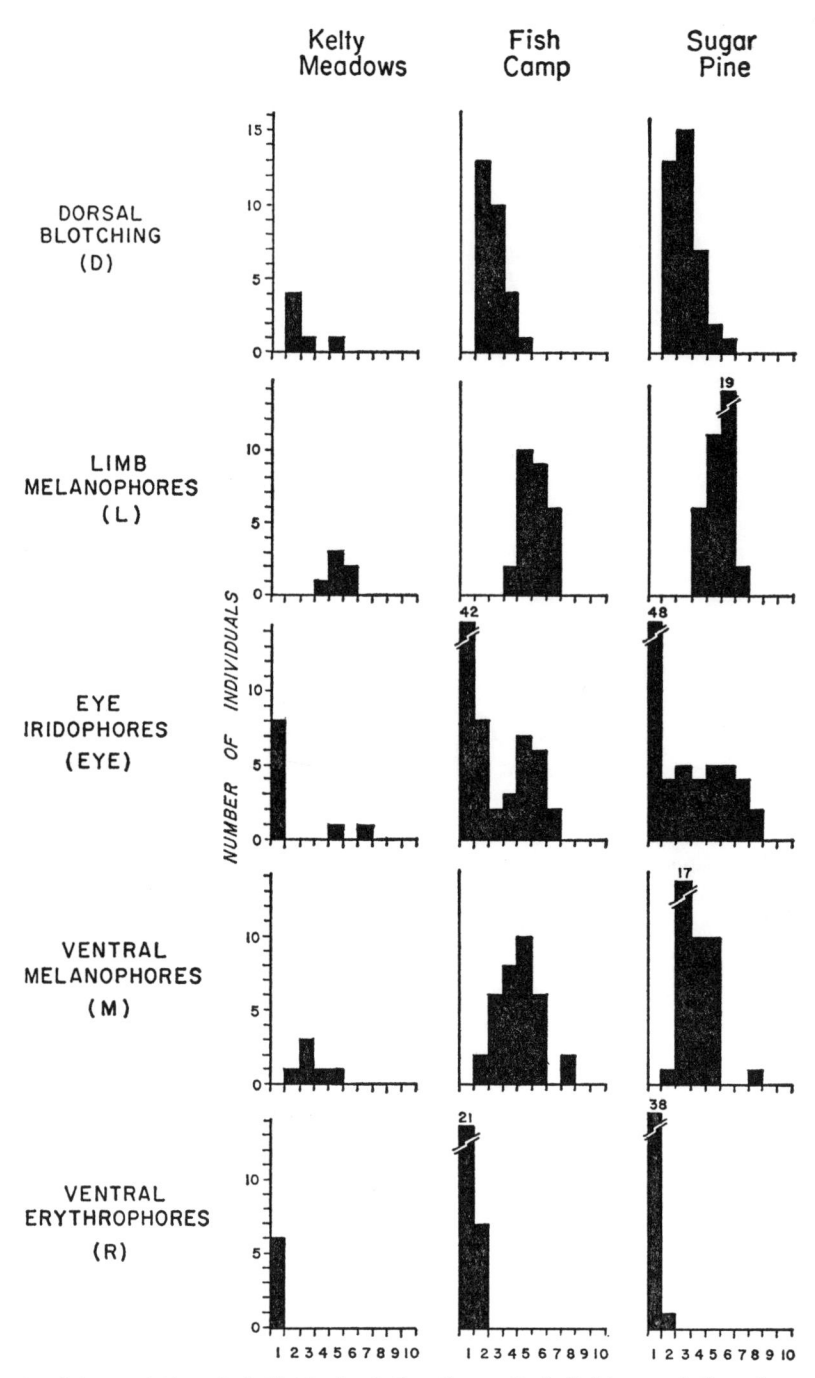

Fig. 12. Color variations in individuals of *Ensatina eschscholtzi* in populations from various localities of Bass Lake region. Horizontal axis: value of each characteristic for each individual. Left and right eye iridophore development values included in same graph. Vertical axis: number of individuals for each series.

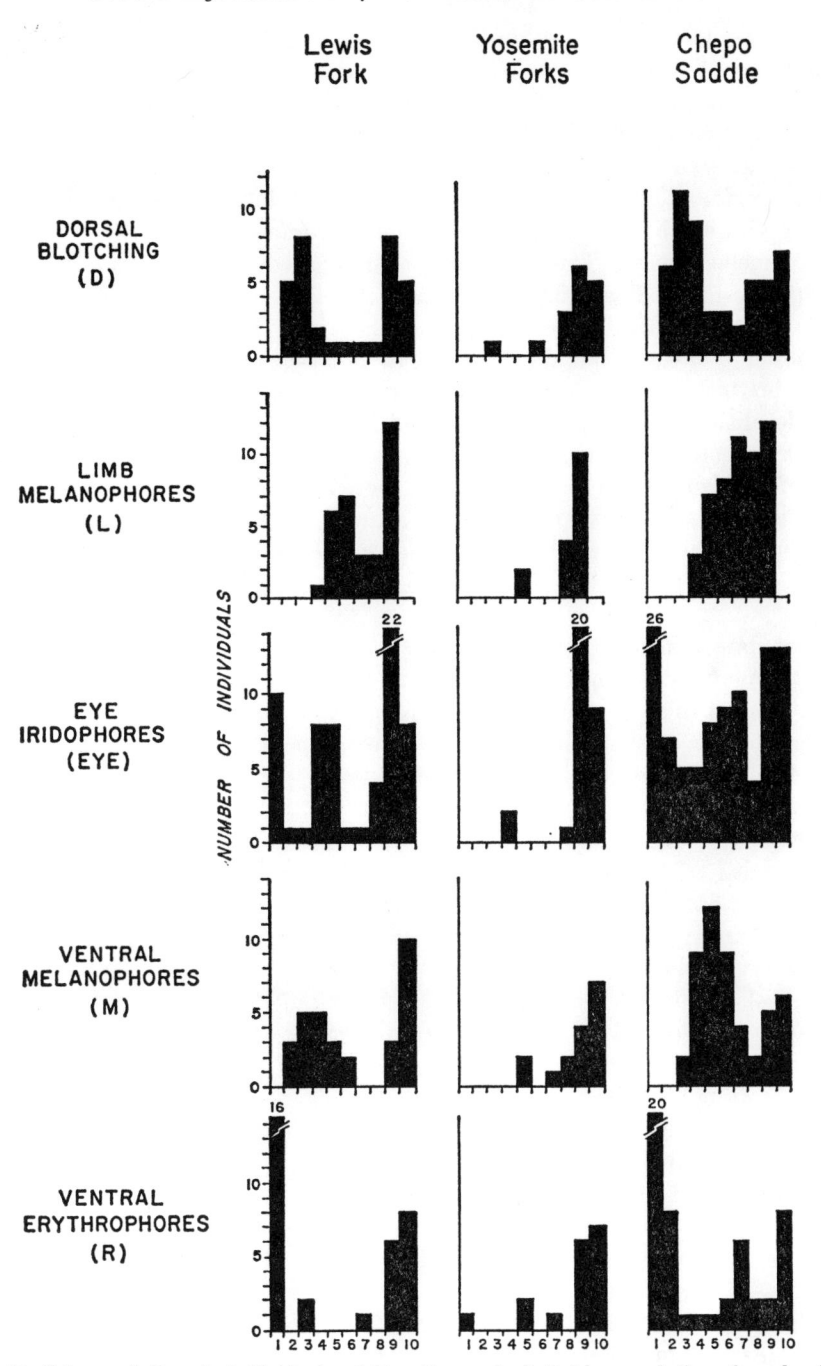

Fig. 13. Color variations in individuals of *Ensatina eschscholtzi* in populations from localities in Bass Lake region. Horizontal axis: value of each characteristic for each individual. Left and right eye iridophore development values included in same graph. Vertical axis: number of individuals for each series.

sistently far more than any *xanthoptica*. *Xanthoptica* at Yosemite Forks, Lewis Fork Creek, Oakhurst, and Miami Creek localities lack ventral melanophores almost entirely, with values ranging from 7 to 10, most at 9 and 10. In fact, many *xanthoptica* show a striking lack of melanophores over the entire body surface. There is some degree of correlation between melanophore development on the ventral surface and dorsal blotching. Ventral melanophores are inversely correlated with erythrophore development on all surfaces.

Limb melanophores: The degree of melanophore development is highly variable in *platensis* of the Bass Lake region, and this is also true of the *platensis* found in the Calaveras Big Trees region. This character is not only variable from one individual to the next, but also from one limb to the next. The hind limbs generally have more melanophores than the front limbs. *Xanthoptica* is much less variable in all localities of this region. This lack of melanophores on the limbs is consistent with the general reduction in these pigment cells throughout the Sierran populations of *xanthoptica*. In the hybrid zone, there appears no bimodality in the values of this characteristic, and there is only a rough positive correlation between limb melanophores and dorsal blotching or lack of ventral erythrophores.

CONCLUSION AND SUMMARY

These data indicate that in the Sierra Nevada, *xanthoptica* populations meet *platensis* populations in a relatively narrow zone of hybridization between 3000 and 4000 feet (figs. 7 and 10). Local topography and climatic conditions affect the type of vegetation which occurs between these two elevations, and this in turn determines the position of contact between the two races.

Xanthoptica and *platensis* are sympatric with little evidence of introgression. Intermediate forms found in the zone of contact have been few in number. The total number of specimens studied in the Calaveras Big Trees and Bass Lake regions was 312, of which 184 were *platensis*, 103 *xanthoptica*, and 25 hybrids. This indicates that approximately 8 percent of all individuals collected within the regions of this study are hybrids.[3]

The color pattern characters show varying degrees of variability in *xanthoptica* and *platensis* populations. Furthermore, these characters also show a strong bimodality in the hybrid zones. In order of degree of variability and bimodality, from high to low, the five characters can be listed as follows: (1) ventral erythrophores, (2) dorsal blotching, (3) eye iridophores, (4) ventral melanophores, and (5) limb melanophore development.

In both regions, Calaveras Big Trees and Bass Lake, the geographic distribution of phenotypic characters studied is quite similar. They both show a relatively narrow zone of hybridization. The evidence of strong bimodality in certain characteristics, such as dorsal blotching and ventral erythrophores, demonstrates the high degree of discontinuity between the gene pools of adjacent *xanthoptica* and *platensis* populations. This situation exists in both regions studied and supports the idea that there are partial reproductive isolating barriers between the two races.

An alternative idea is that hybrids and hybrid backcrosses are at a much

---

[3] Hybrids as defined in this study are arbitrarily set for mean values between 4.7 and 7.2.

greater selective disadvantage than the parental stocks. This disadvantage may be related to cryptic coloration, physiological adaptation, or some aspects of courtship behavior.

SOUTHERN CALIFORNIA POPULATIONS
GENERAL ASPECTS

Populations of the blotched races, *croceater* and *klauberi* or their intergrades, are found in disjunct pockets from the Tehachapi Mountains in Kern County south to the Mexican border. There appears to be a distinct gap between *croceater* populations found at Fort Tejon and Mount Pinos in Kern County and populations of the unblotched race *eschscholtzi* which occur in the Santa Monica Mountains of Los Angeles County 50 miles to the south, and the mountains around Ojai about 30 miles to the southwest of Fort Tejon. There also exists a gap between *croceater* populations of the Tehachapi Mountains and *croceater-klauberi* intergrades of the San Bernardino Mountains about 120 miles east of Fort Tejon.

The populations of the unblotched subspecies *eschscholtzi* meet the blotched populations of *croceater-klauberi* in the San Bernardino Mountains around San Gorgonio Mountain. In the one locality, Sawmill Canyon, which is an upper tributary of the San Gorgonio River above Banning, *eschscholtzi* meets *croceater-klauberi* in an extremely narrow zone of hybridization (fig. 14).

About 50 miles south of the San Gorgonio Mountain region is the Palomar Mountain region. On mountains near Palomar Observatory, unblotched populations of the subspecies *eschscholtzi* meet the blotched populations of the subspecies *klauberi*, again in extremely narrow zones of hybridization. In some cases, there exists exidence of considerable overlap and sympatry between the blotched and unblotched populations with little evidence of hybridization and introgression (figs. 15 and 16).

About 30 miles southeast of Palomar Mountain there are *klauberi* populations in the Cuyamaca Mountains around Julian and Cuyamaca Ranch State Park. In these localities the blotched populations appear to be relatively free of genetic influence from unblotched populations. Martin B. Ruggles (1969) reported that one *eschscholtzi* × *klauberi* hybrid was collected by W. O. Gregg in 1942 at Cuyamaca Lake, and is now in the Los Angeles County Museum with the number 301. (R. Stebbins, personal communication).

In both the Palomar and Cuyamaca mountains, an adequate sample of *Ensatina* was analyzed for both color patterns. Emphasis was placed on the hybrid zones around Palomar Mountain, specifically at (1) Cedar Creek near Jeff Valley and (2) Dyche Valley and (3) Will Valley about 3 miles ESE of Jeff Valley (figs. 15 and 16).

SAN GORGONIO MOUNTAIN REGION

General description of the region.—The San Gorgonio Mountain Region, as defined in this study, is located about 60 miles east of Los Angeles in the San Bernardino Mountains (fig. 5). This region is approximately 20 miles long and 30 miles wide and includes the following major localities at which *Ensatina* populations were studied: (1) Crystal Creek (CCSB), (2) Forest Home or Mill Creek

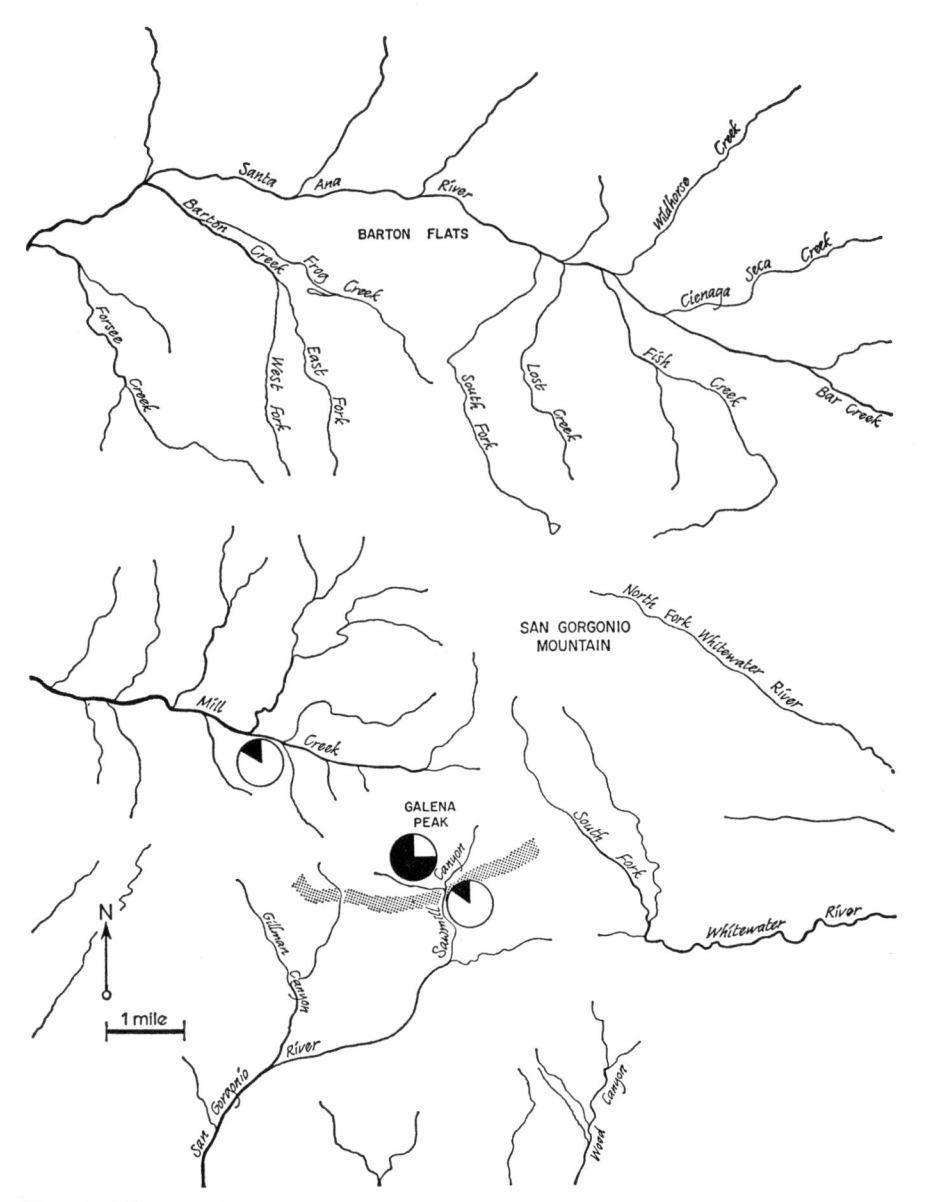

Fig. 14. Color variations in populations of *Ensatina eschscholtzi* in the San Gorgonio Mountain region. Stippled area represents possible hybrid zone. Pie diagrams are mean values for all four characteristics of the entire population for that locality, and expressed in percentages of 360°. An open circle would represent a hypothetical "pure" *eschscholtzi* population, completely free of genetic influence from *croceater-klauberi* intergrade populations. A solid circle would represent a hypothetical "pure" *croceater-klauberi* population, completely free from genetic influence from *eschscholtzi* populations.

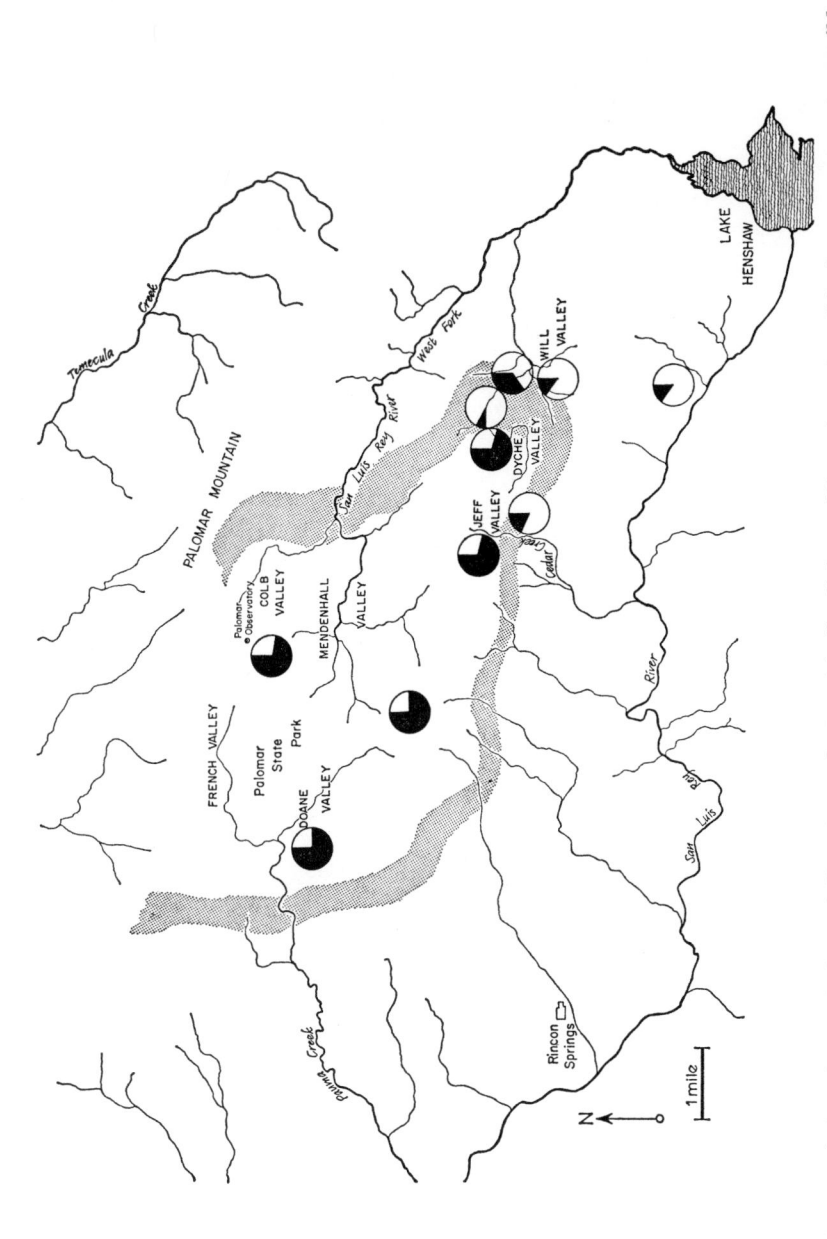

Fig. 15. Color variations in populations of *Ensatina eschscholtzi* in the Palomar Mountain region. Stipple area represents possible hybrid zone. Pie diagrams are mean values for all four characteristics of the entire population for that locality, and expressed in percentage of 360°. An open circle would represent a hypothetical "pure" *eschscholtzi* population completely free from genetic influence from *klauberi* populations. A solid circle would represent a hypothetical "pure" *klauberi* population completely free of genetic influence from *eschscholtzi* populations.

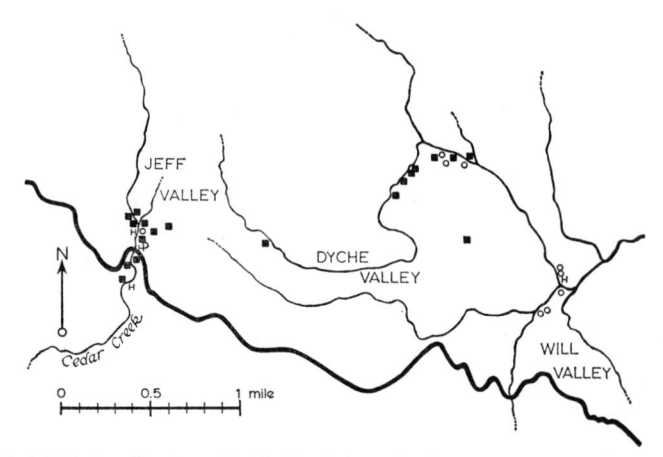

Fig. 16. Detailed distribution of individuals in hybrid zone of Palomar Mountain region. Solid squares represent typical *klauberi*, open circles represent typical *eschscholtzi*, and H = presumed F₁ hybrids. Not all individuals were plotted on map. Note degree of overlap of blotched and unblotched individuals.

(FHSB), and (3) Sawmill Canyon (SCSB). The letters (SB) stand for San Bernardino County, in which these localities are found. These localities range from Forest Home along Mill Creek at 5200 feet in elevation to Sawmill Canyon at 6300 feet and Mill Creek at 6600 feet (see fig. 14).

The major stream drainages include Crystal Creek, which drains from the San Bernardino Mountains north of Big Bear Lake northward into the Mojave Desert near Lucerne. South of Big Bear Lake, and southwest of San Gorgonio Mountain, Mill Creek drains west into the Santa Ana River. Due south of San Gorgonio Mountain, this stream in Sawmill Canyon, headwaters of the San Gorgonio River, flows south to meet the San Gorgonio River, which flows east to Whitewater River in the Coachella Valley.

These stream drainages are deeply cut and are characterized by steep, rocky canyon walls, sparse, arid vegetation along the ridges, and narrow strips of pine-cedar forests in the canyon bottoms above 5500 feet. Below 5500 feet, the pine-cedar association gives way to oak forests and chaparral.

Although the number of inches of precipitation per year is moderate at these elevations, the region is generally arid because the precipitation is so infrequent. Thus much of the vegetation is of a desert form and the coniferous forests are in pockets on tops of mountains or in small narrow strips along stream drainages. As a consequence, suitable habitat for *Ensatina* is uncommon, being restricted to small pockets.

Color analysis and habitat description (Fig. 17).—

1. Crystal Creek series (CCSB): In a steep stream drainage, *Ensatina eschscholtzi croceater-klauberi* has been found along an ancient, narrow and permanent stream called Crystal Creek. Recently, quarrying above the stream has buried part of this fine locality in about three feet of rock and gravel. A detailed habitat description can be found in Stebbins (1949).

The dorsal blotching seems to be as irregular in this population as in the

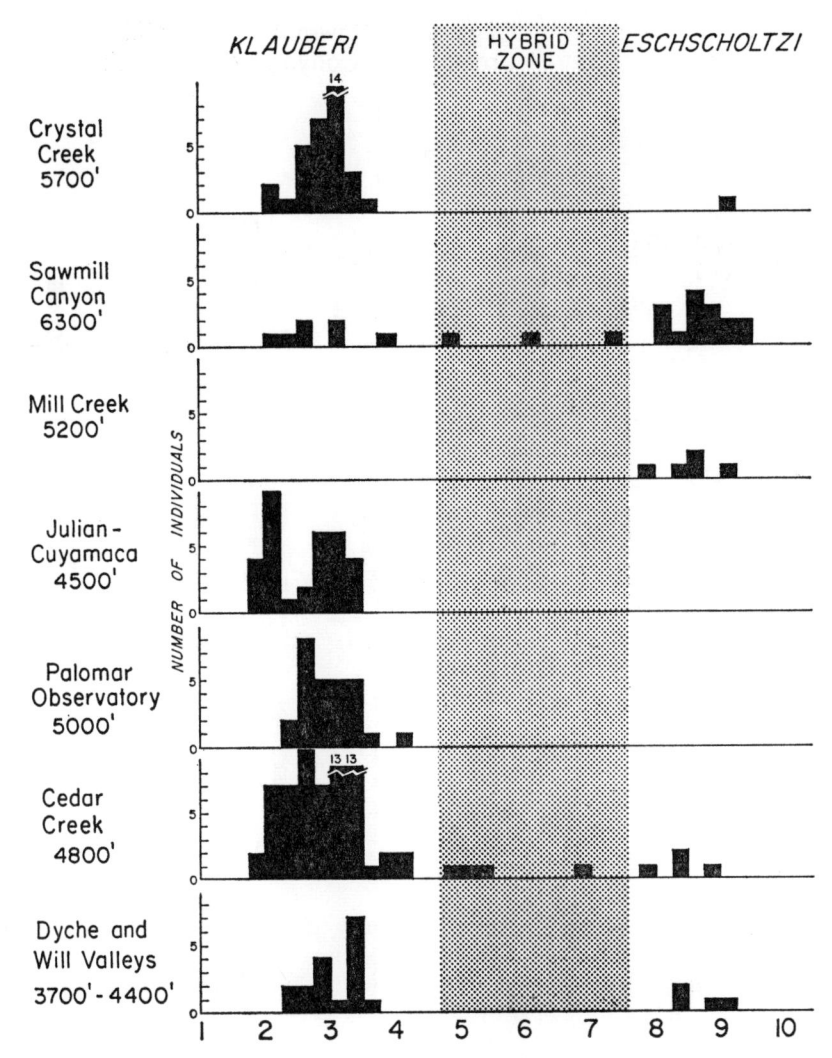

Fig. 17. Color variations in individuals of *Ensatina eschscholtzi* in Southern California populations. Horizontal axis: mean value for each individual for four characteristics (parotoid blotching, dorsal blotching, limb melanophores, and ventral melanophores). Vertical axis: number of individuals for each series.

blotched individuals found in Sawmill Canyon (fig. 18). In addition, in the blotching of the Crystal Creek specimens there were often found scattered melanophores, which seem to be a characteristic of hybrid backcrosses. It is suggested that there may be some genetic influence of *eshscholtzi* from the direction of the Lake Arrowhead region where the unblotched form was collected earlier by R. Stebbins.

2. Mill Creek series (FHSB): Only five unblotched *Ensatina* of the subspecies *eschscholtzi* were studied from this creek drainage. All seemed to show some irregularities in dorsal melanic pigmentation, which indicates possible introgres-

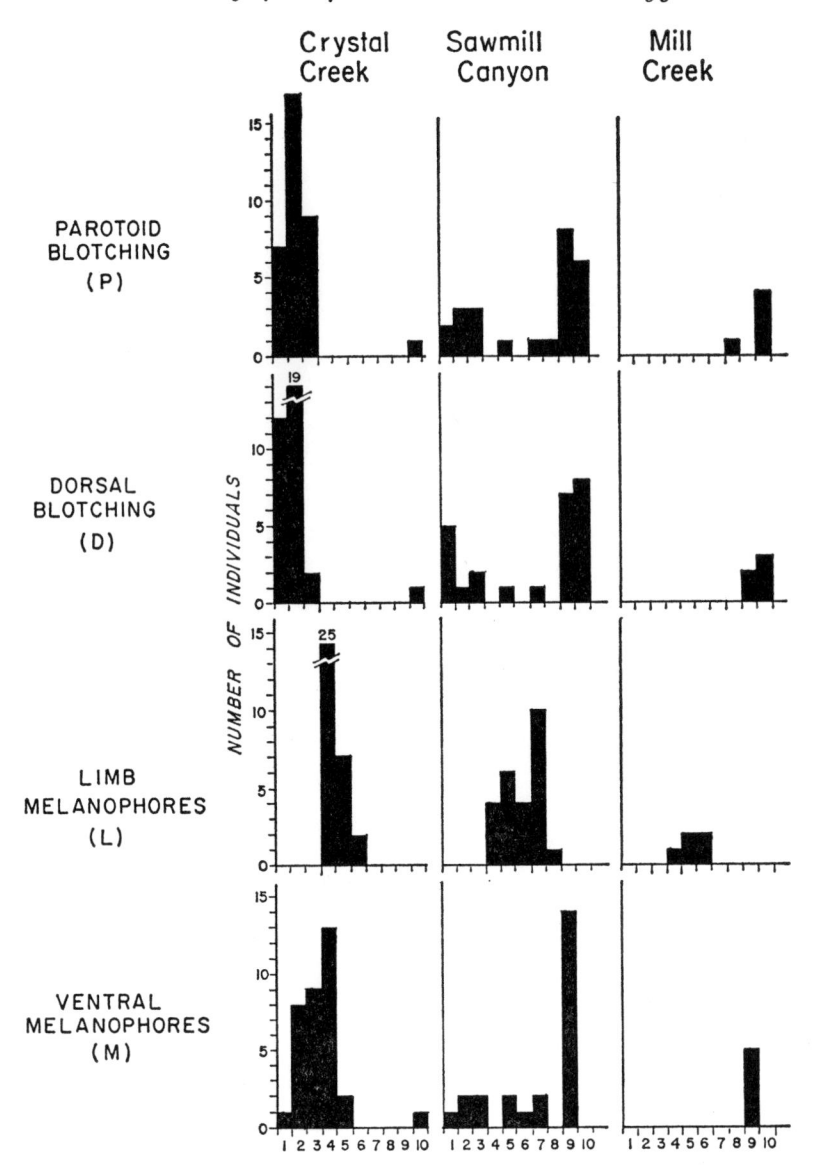

Fig. 18. Color variations in individuals of *Ensatina eschscholtzi* in populations from various localities of San Gorgonio Mountain region. Horizontal axis: value of each characteristic for each individual. Vertical axis: number of individuals for each series.

sion from a blotched population that may be at higher elevations. More collecting is necessary in this habitat, which is relatively marginal for *Ensatina*, for a clear picture to emerge.

3. Sawmill Canyon series (SCSB): At a point one mile north of the junction of Burnt and Sawmill canyons (elevation 6200 feet), the stream in Sawmill Canyon splits into two tributaries, one coming from the west, the other from north by northeast. Above 6200 feet seven typical *croceater-klauberi* were col-

lected. Below 6200 feet fifteen *eschscholtzi* were found, one presumed hybrid and two hybrid backcrosses.

In general, vegetation in this canyon is highly variable. No one particular species of tree is predominant. Along the canyon bottom above 6000 feet elevation, the banks along the rocky stream are covered with moderate stands of Incense Cedar, whereas on the steep slope the Big Cone Spruce (*Pseudotsuga macrocarpa*) and Coulter Pine or Big Cone Pine (*Pinus coulteri*) predominate in patches. In other portions of the canyon bottom and along the steep slopes, Canyon Oak (*Quercus chrysolepsis*) is found variously scattered and in clumps. This oak species forms a heavy stand around the stream junction at 6200 feet, especially over the east-facing slopes. In the tributary flowing from the west, the heavy cover along the bottom is primarily White Alder (*Alnus rhombifolia*) and oak. Below 6000 feet the canyon bottom and steep slopes are covered primarily by stands of Canyon Oak with a few scattered Incense Cedar.

Apparently there is an extremely narrow zone of hybridization in this canyon. All *eschscholtzi* found south of the 6200-foot elevation at the stream juncture had mean values of 8.00 and 9.25, and all *croceater-klauberi* possessed mean values of 2.00 to 3.75. In a 200-foot space between the blotched and unblotched forms were found two individuals, one with a mean value of 5.75 (presumed hybrid) and a blotched specimen with a value of 4.75 (possible backcross of hybrid with *croceater-klauberi* parent). Downstream about 0.3 mile, an *eschscholtzi* was collected which had somewhat irregular melanic patches along the dorsal and lateral surfaces. This specimen turned out to have a mean value of 7.0 and is thought to be from a backcross of a hybrid with an *eschscholtzi* parent.

GEOGRAPHIC CORRELATION OF COLORS

Parotoid surfaces: The blotch over the parotoid surface of a "pure" *croceater-klauberi* is fairly rectilinear and extends across the back of the head connecting the lateral surfaces. In the unblotched form, of course, this entire surface is covered with a rather uniformly mixed network of melonophores and erythrophores. In the presumed hybrid (CWB 100), there is an irregular pattern of melanic blotches and mixing of melanophores over the entire parotoid surface. It is not surprising to find that in CWB 99, a presumed hybrid backcross, the blotches on the lateral parotoid region are not connected by a continuous dorsal rectilinear blotch, but are separated by an irregular mid-dorsal melanophore development. Furthermore, the blotch is not made up entirely of xanthophores but has a scattering of melanophores, which give the blotch an irregular appearance.

In the section on blotching in *klauberi* (below p. 43) the degree of irregularity in parotoid blotching is used as a diagnostic characteristic for genetic influence from unblotched populations.

Dorsal blotching: Apparently there is more genetic introgression into the blotched populations than was previously thought. Many of the blotched individuals both in Crystal Creek and Sawmill Canyon have rather irregular blotches with a scattering of melanophores in the blotches. As we shall see, it is the so-called hybrid backcross near zones of hybridization which exhibit these irregularities in areas of contact between *klauberi* and *eschscholtzi* further south. The blotched *klauberi* in regions relatively isolated from unblotched *eschscholtzi* have highly rectilinear blotches which are nearly devoid of melanic patches, which is to say that the melanophores and erythrophores (or xanthophores) are separated.

The unblotched subspecies *eschscholtzi* shows little evidence of introgression from blotched populations either in Mill Creek[4] or Sawmill Canyon specimens. Thus the fairly uniform coloration in these individuals may have a high selective value, but this would be difficult to determine. Additional specimens are needed to support this view.

The one hybrid between blotched and unblotched forms found in Sawmill Canyon has an unusual dorsal color pattern. There are irregular patches of melanophores over the body and tail with an "elongate blotch over each epibranchial portion extending back over the foreleg," (Stebbins, 1962). Similar patches were found in CWB 87, the *eschscholtzi* presumed to be a hybrid backcross.

Limb melanophores: There is not much variation in the degree of melanic development in the distal portion of the limbs. Values range from 4 to 8, with the blotched forms having heavier melanophore development, more concentrated in the dorsal portion, whereas the unblotched forms have fewer melanophores, which are more widely scattered over the limb surfaces.

Ventral melanophores: As in the dorsal blotching, there is a distinct bimodality in the degree of ventral melanophore development in Sawmill Canyon. There is a high degree of variability in the number and position of melanophores in the blotched forms; however, in *eschscholtzi* melanophores are almost entirely absent from ventral surfaces of head, body and tail. Most *eschscholtzi* possess a very few around the ventral margin of the lower jaw.

PALOMAR MOUNTAIN REGION

General description of the region.—The Palomar Mountain Region, as defined by this study, is located 90 miles southeast of Los Angeles, and 40 miles north by northeast of San Diego (fig. 5). This region is approximately 10 miles long and 10 miles wide and includes the following localities: (1) Palomar Observatory (POSD), (2) Cedar Creek (CKSD), (3) Dyche Valley (DVSD), and (4) Will Valley (WVSD). About 25 miles south-southeast of Palomar Mountain are two other localities included in this portion of the study as a basis for comparison: (5) Julian (JUSD) and (6) Cuyamaca State Park (CUSD). The letters SD stand for San Diego County. Localities in the Palomar Mountain Region range from San Luis Rey River at 2600 feet to 5300 feet near Palomar Observatory (fig. 15).

The major stream drainages include (1) San Luis Rey River which drains Mendenhall Valley and Palomar Mountain first to the east via Lake Henshaw and then to the west, (2) Cedar Creek which drains Jeff Valley southwest to San Luis Rey River, (3) Pauma Creek which drains French and Doane Valley, of Palomar State Park, to the west and eventually joins the San Luis Rey River.

---

[4] Blotched forms have yet to be obtained from Mill Creek drainage. However, there is a population in Sawmill Canyon just over a high ridge. Future collecting will probably reveal blotched forms along the upper portions of Mill Creek.

These stream drainages are deeply cut in some places and less so in others, but in general are of rapid flow and steep after leaving the level upper reaches of Palomar Mountain. Above 4500 feet, the mountains are irregularly covered with heavy groves of Incense Cedar, Big Cone Pine and Black Oak (*Quercus kelloggii*). There are many open areas or meadows, some of which are covered by chaparral, while others are covered with grass and herbs.

The precipitation level on this particular mountain range is quite high, being over 40 inches per year at Palomar State Park. As a consequence, the forests in some localities (e.g., Palomar State Park and some canyon bottoms) are quite heavy. This is mostly true on north-facing slopes. On the southern exposures, above 4500 feet, there exists suitable habitat for *Ensatina*. Rotten logs and heavy leaf litter are abundant above 4000 feet.

Below 4500 feet, the vegetation changes abruptly, generally due to the steepness of the slopes. Pine-oak-cedar associations are replaced by oak-chaparral covered hillsides. In the oak and chaparral, leaf litter is much thinner than in pine-cedar associations, and rock outcroppings are much more evident. It is at this elevation (4000–4500 feet) that the blotched and unblotched populations of *Ensatina* are in juxtaposition.

Color analysis and habitat descriptions.—

1. Palomar Observatory series (POSD): Southwest of the observatory (5000–5500 feet) are areas variously covered by heavy stands of Incense Cedar, medium cover of pine, scattered pine-oak forests, open grasslands and chaparral. In this locality, around Palomar Observatory Campground, the hills are gently sloping, but level areas are not uncommon.

The mean values of the four characters studied in a sample of 27 *klauberi* ranged from 2.25 to 4.00 with a mean of 2.85. There was some evidence of introgression from *eschscholtzi* populations as blotches were not as regular (or rectilinear) as in the Julian series (mean value of 2.50).

The range in values of hue, value, and chroma are somewhat less than *klauberi* from Cedar Creek. Hue ranges from 15.0 to 20.0, value from 6 to 8, and chroma from 4 to 10.

2. Cedar Creek series (CKSD): Cedar Creek is a small tributary of the San Luis Rey River, which drains Jeff Valley. In that portion of the stream drainage studied, the stream first travels through a gently sloping west portion of Jeff Valley, a fairly large open grassy area surrounded by Incense Cedar and Big Cone Pine. The stream then passes through a heavy stand of Incense Cedar just before it reaches the paved highway from Palomar Observatory to Lake Henshaw. After it passes under the highway, it begins to drop more rapidly from 4700 feet down to 3000 feet where it flows into Pauma Valley and the San Luis Rey River.

In the dense Incense Cedar grove just above the highway at about 4900 feet elevation, a large population of *klauberi* was located. A total of 76 blotched forms was collected and analyzed, along with 5 unblotched *eschscholtzi* and 2 distinct hybrids (CWB 676). Two of the blotched forms were apparent backcrosses with the parental subspecies. The hybrids were very distinctive in coloration and melanic distribution. The background was a salmon color, and over the dorsal surface was an irregular network of melanic patches and blotches. Individual melanophores were scattered throughout the dorsal surfaces. One of the presumed backcrosses (possibly hybrid × *klauberi*) had distinct blotches but with irregular edges (not rectilinear) and melanophores scattered through the blotches. The color was slightly salmon but lighter than the hybrid. None of the *eschscholtzi* resembled a backcross such as the example from Sawmill Canyon (CWB 87). This hybrid had only a few ventral melanophores, which were on the edges of the lower jaw.

One outstanding characteristic of the blotched individuals in this locality is the high degree of variability of hue, value, and chroma of the color of the blotches. Some specimens were a deep reddish orange (15.0 YR 6/8),[5] and others were almost as cream white as in the *croceater-klauberi* intergrade (25.0 Y 8/2) (see fig. 4). No other population of *klauberi* was observed to be as variable in these characteristics as the one in Cedar Creek,[6] but samples from other localities have been small. It is proposed here that this variability was due to the influence of *eschscholtzi* genetic introgression.

3. Dyche (DVSD) and Will Valley (WVSD) series: About one mile southeast of Jeff Valley is Dyche Valley. From Dyche Valley a stream drains southeast about two miles to Will Valley. Dyche Valley is a large open meadow about half a mile wide and one mile long, surrounded by open stands of Coulter Pine. Along the stream to Will Valley there is a medium stand of Incense Cedar, mixed with Big Cone Pine and Black Oak. At about 4400 feet, the Incense Cedar gives way to a mixture of Coulter Pine, Black Oak, and Canyon Oak. It is at this point that an overlap between *eschscholtzi* and *klauberi* occurs. Below 4400 feet, the northeast facing slopes are covered with a medium stand of Coulter Pine, Black Oak, and Canyon Oak interspersed with areas of chaparral. On the southwest facing slopes, chaparral is predominant.

The 17 blotched and 13 unblotched individuals collected between Dyche and Will valleys are typical for their subspecies, with little or no evidence of introgression, with the exception of two individuals. Usually the blotched *klauberi* are found above 4000 feet, and the unblotched *eschscholtzi* are found below 4400 feet, there being about 0.2 mile overlap or sympatry (see figs. 15 and 16). A distinct hybrid was located about one mile downstream from the nearest *klauberi*, at a 3700 foot elevation, near Will Valley. This indicated that there is probably an even greater overlap. No *klauberi* have yet been found at Will Valley, but, based on the fact that the hybrid was collected at that locality, the blotched forms may exist there.

4. Julian (JUSD) and Cuyamaca State Park (CUSD) series: The mountain range named Cuyamaca, which runs from Julian south to Descanso through Cuyamaca State Park, is covered in parts by heavy to light stands of Incense Cedar and Coulter Pine, Black Oak and Cayon Oak, and in other areas there are

---

[5] In 15.0 YR 6/8: 15.0 = hue, YR = yellow red; 6 = value; 8 = chroma. From *Munsell Book of Color*.

[6] Stebbins (1949) found one individual at Cuyamaca State Park which was "pale orange yellow laterally to capucine orange" (22.5 Y 8/4).

open meadows and chaparral-covered hillsides, depending on the exposure. The range is not very high and consists mostly of gentle rolling hills, which border the lower desert to the east. Generally the north- and east-facing slopes and some of the canyon bottoms are the most heavily forested.

The blotched subspecies *klauberi* has been collected in this region, and these individuals seem to show the most rectilinearity in the blotches, the narrowest range of hue, value, and chroma, and the heaviest ventral melanophore development. For these reasons, these populations have been selected as a standard for *klauberi* and are thought to be least influenced by introgression from *eschscholtzi*.

The mean value of the four characters ranges from 1.75 to 3.25, with a median of about 2.50. Blotches are highly regular, and the dorsal head blotch is most often continuous, joining the parotoid region. Hue, value, and chroma also have narrow ranges from 15.0 YR 5/8 to 20.0 Y 6/10.

GEOGRAPHIC CORRELATION OF COLORS

Parotoid surfaces (P): In the reference *klauberi* populations from Julian and Cuyamaca State Park the parotoid regions are generally joined by a continuous rectilinear blotch.[7] Other *klauberi* populations found at Cedar Creek and Palomar Observatory showed a great variability in this dorsal head blotching. For this reason it is thought that there is greater genetic introgression from *eschscholtzi* into the *klauberi* population in the Palomar Mountains than in the Cuyamaca Mountains. Values range from 1 to 4 in the Palomar Mountains with a mean value of 1.81, whereas in the Cuyamaca Mountains, values range from 1 to 2 with a mean value of 1.36 (fig. 19).

Dorsal blotching (D): As in the parotoid surfaces, the dorsal blotching is more rectilinear in the populations of Cuyamaca Mountains than in the Palomar Mountain populations. There is also greater evidence of melanophores within the blotches in the latter than in the former. This apparently indicates greater variability and introgression from *eschscholtzi* populations into *klauberi* populations in the Palomar Mountains. This is particularly evident in the Cedar Creek series where the *eschscholtzi* and *klauberi* meet.
eschscholtzi and *klauberi* meet.

Hue, value and chroma of dorsal colors: It is clear that in the Cuyamaca Mountain populations, *klauberi* exhibits less variability in the quality of color than *klauberi* in Cedar Creek (see fig. 4).

MISCELLANEOUS SOUTHERN CALIFORNIA REGIONS

All other *klauberi* and *eschscholtzi* analyzed from other isolated localities in Riverside and San Diego counties fall within the normal range of values for those subspecies. The sample size of these individuals is small (usually a single individual for each locality). For this reason no definite statements can be made at this time.

---

[7] The value 1 was used to designate a continuous rectilinear blotch and 2 a broken blotch. Nineteen individuals at Julian and Cuyamaca have the value 1, whereas only eleven had the value 2.

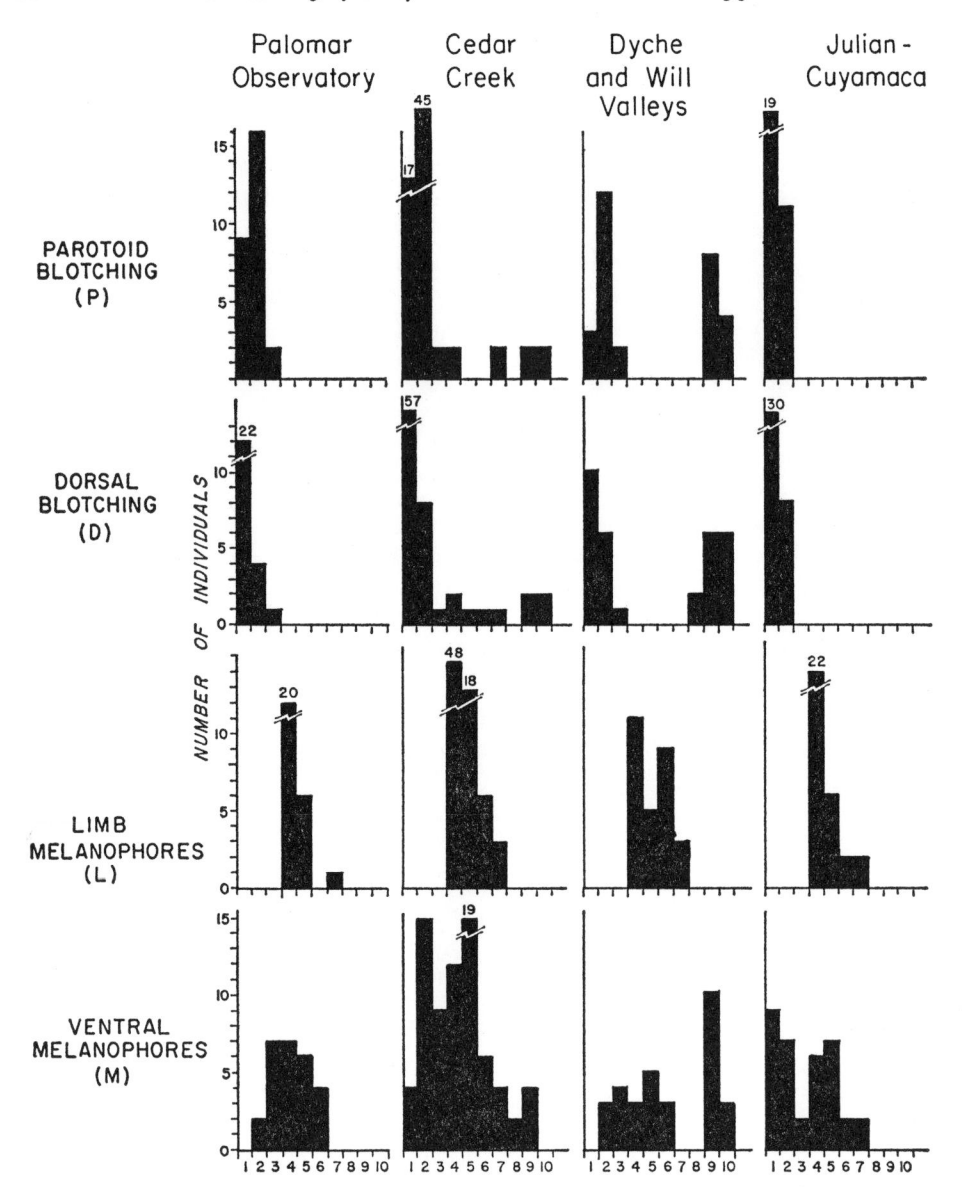

Fig. 19. Color variations in individuals of *Ensatina eschscholtzi* in populations from various localities of Palomar Mountain region. Horizontal axis: value of each characteristic for each individual. Vertical axis: number of individuals for each series.

Conclusion and Summary

These data indicate that in the San Bernardino Mountains, *eschscholtzi* populations meet *croceater-klauberi* intergrades in an extremely narrow zone of hybridization at 6200 feet in Sawmill Canyon. It is suspected that the blotched and unblotched subspecies also hybridize somewhere between Lake Arrowhead and Crystal Creek, based on the degree of variability in the Crystal Creek Series.

These data also indicate that in the mountains around the Palomar Observatory, *eschscholtzi* populations overlap with *klauberi* populations with some evidence for limited hybridization and introgression. There is a distinct difference between the vegetation in typical *klauberi* habitat as compared to the vegetation found in the habitat of *eschscholtzi*. Out of a total of 260 individuals studied from Southern California, 206 were blotched forms (*klauberi* and *croceater-klauberi*), 46 were unblotched *eschscholtzi*, 4 were hybrids (presumably close to F_1 hybrids), and 4 were apparent backcrosses. This indicates that approximately 3.5 percent of all individuals from this area were hybrids, based on the color characteristics analyzed in this paper.

Both *klauberi* and *eschscholtzi* populations show varying degrees of variability in the color pattern characters studied. Again, as in the Sierra Nevada, some of these characters show a strong bimodality in the hybrid zones. In order of degree of variability (from low to high) and bimodality (from high to low) the five characters can be listed as follows: (1) dorsal blotching (2) parotoid blotching (3) ventral melanophores and (4) limb melanophores.

Both Sawmill Canyon of San Bernardino County and Cedar Creek of San Diego County, where the blotched and unblotched populations meet, show an extremely narrow zone of hybridization. In fact, in both the Cedar Creek and Dyche Valley localities, there is evidence of overlap and little hybridization or introgression (figs. 16 and 17). There is evidence of strong bimodality in certain characteristics and a high degree of discontinuity between the gene pools of adjacent *klauberi* and *eschscholtzi* populations. The blotched form *klauberi* shows a higher degree of variability in hue, value, and chroma in the Cedar Creek population than in the Cuyamaca Mountain populations. The situation which exists in both the Sierra Nevada and Southern California mountains strongly supports the idea that there may be major reproductive incompatibility between the inland blotched and coastal unblotched races.

It is very unlikely that so many contact zones between blotched and unblotched forms could have occurred only in recent years. Therefore, these populations have probably been in contact for hundreds, possibly thousands of years, without swamping of gene pools. This, plus the rarity of hybrids, stresses the point that the reproductive isolating barriers, though not complete, are nevertheless substantial and effective in preventing massive genetic introgression.

Eschscholtzi examined from several Southern California localities have some irregularities in their dorsal melanic pigmentation. These localities include (1) Soldier Creek near Crystal Lake and Big Pines Recreation Area in Los Angeles County, (2) Mill Creek and Sawmill Canyon in San Bernardino County, (3) Indian Creek west of San Jacinto Mountain in Riverside County,[8] and (4) Cedar Creek near Jeff Valley and Dyche and Will valleys in San Diego County. This would be expected in populations from San Bernardino, Riverside, and San Diego counties which are in contact with blotched populations. However, no blotched form has yet been found in the San Gabriel Mountains, or in the Soldier Creek and Big Pines areas. Two explanations may be offered for the failure to detect

---

[8] Recent additions to the MVZ collections have been donated by Michael C. Long of Monterey Park.

blotched populations in the San Gabriel Mountains: (1) the former blotched populations which may have existed there have been swamped by *eschscholtzi*, or (2) there remain undiscovered pockets occupied by *croceater-klauberi* intergrades.

BIOCHEMICAL ANALYSIS
METHODS AND MATERIALS

It is fully recognized that analysis of genetic divergence leading to reproductive isolation usually involves changes in an entire complex of genetic traits. Therefore it was decided that characteristics in addition to color patterns should be investigated. Blood serum proteins were chosen, not only because they are very likely to be a phenotypic expression of gene loci which are different from those genes for the expression of pigment patterns, but also because serum proteins are probably one step closer to the genetic material (DNA) than are the color patterns. In addition, serum proteins may give the systematist a better perspective of gene flow betwen different populations (Salthe, 1969).

For example, Zweifel (1962) found that two subspecies of the Desert Whiptail Lizard (*Cnemidophorus tigris*) meet in a narrow zone in southwestern New Mexico.. Analysis of color patterns and scutellation showed that only a few individuals indicated some degree of hybridization in a relatively restricted zone. However, studies by Dessauer, Fox, and Pough (1962) on blood plasma proteins indicated a much wider zone of gene flow than shown by Zweifel (1962).

VARIATIONS IN THE SUBSPECIES

The albumin peaks of the northern subspecies of *Ensatina*, particularly *picta*, are both faster and more variable than the peaks of the southern subspecies *eschscholtzi* and *klauberi*. In fact, the full range of values of relative albumin mobility for *picta* is almost as great as for the entire species, including most of the values (Petrakis and Brown, 1970).

When subspecies are compared, it is seen that the distribution lines overlap considerably, a finding that is consistent with the theory of active gene flow among the subspecies and intergrades. For example, on the basis of color pattern analysis and geographic distribution, it has been found that *platensis* intergrades with *oregonensis* to the north and *croceater* to the south. These three subspecies have a number of albumin peaks in common, also suggesting gene flow.

As one progresses southward, the various populations of *Ensatina* gradually drop out various albumin peaks, replacing them with slower ones. The north to south trend, therefore, is one of progressively slower albumin and in addition, fewer peaks in general. *Croceater* shows the smallest variety of albumin peaks, but the sample size is inadequate for a reliable interpretation.

The Sierran *xanthoptica* and *platensis* have considerable overlap. It is most unfortunate that for this study I was unable to analyze any coastal *xanthoptica*. A more detailed comparison of *platensis* and *xanthoptica* populations will be found in the following section.

There is also a sizeable overlap in the *klauberi* and *eschscholtzi* populations in the mountains of Southern California. This surprising finding does not support the genetic divergence idea as interpreted from the color pattern analysis. How-

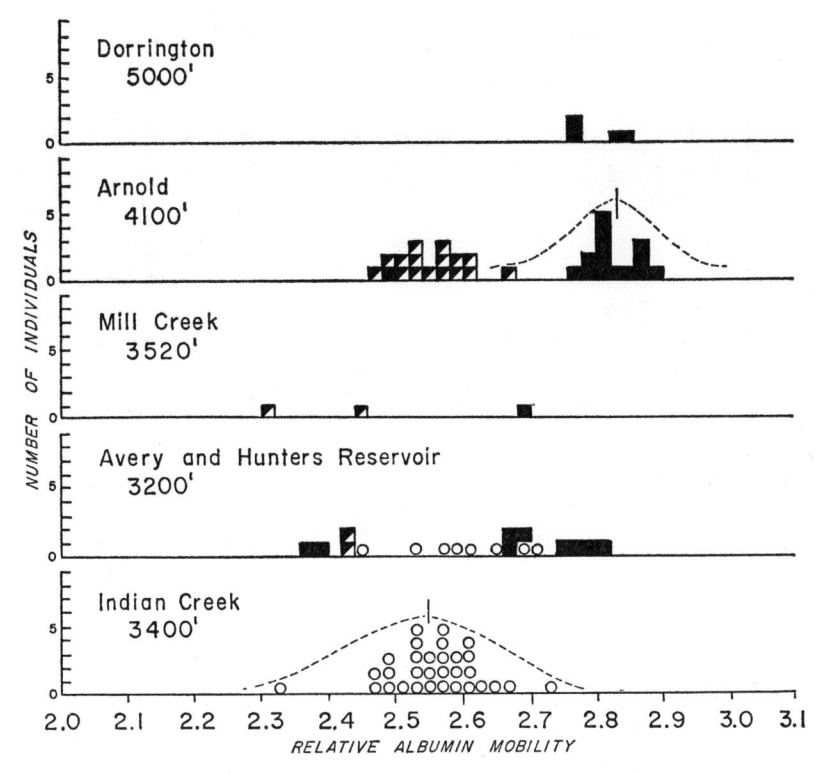

Fig. 20. Relative albumin mobilities for individuals of *Ensatina eschscholtzi* in populations from localities in Calaveras Big Trees region in Sierra Nevada. Horizontal axis: relative mobility of albumin peaks. Vertical axis: number of individuals from each locality. Solid squares represent primary albumin peaks of *platensis*; semi-solid squares represent secondary albumin peaks of *platensis*. Open circles represent primary albumin peaks of *xanthoptica*; circles with dot enclosed represent secondary albumin peak for single *xanthoptica* from Mountain Ranch, 1134 foot elevation. Note (1) the similarity of mean values for primary albumin peaks of *exanthoptica* to secondary albumin peaks of *platensis* sample from Arnold which is considered a reference population; (2) degree of variability in hybrid zone of population at Avery and Hunters Reservoir.

ever, *klauberi* albumins fall *between* clusters of *eschscholtzi* albumins and possess only a few common peaks.

ANALYSIS OF THE HYBRID ZONES

CALAVERAS BIG TREES REGION

There is some evidence for subspecific differences in albumin mobilities as indicated by graph in figure 20. For primary peaks only, there is a distinct difference between the population at Arnold (all *platensis*) and the population at Indian Creek (all *xanthoptica*). However, the population at Arnold possesses a high frequency of secondary peaks corresponding to the same mobility as the primary peaks in the *xanthoptica* population. This may indicate genetic introgression from the *xanthoptica* populations at lower elevations; however, data from Bass Lake Region do not strongly support this idea (fig. 21).

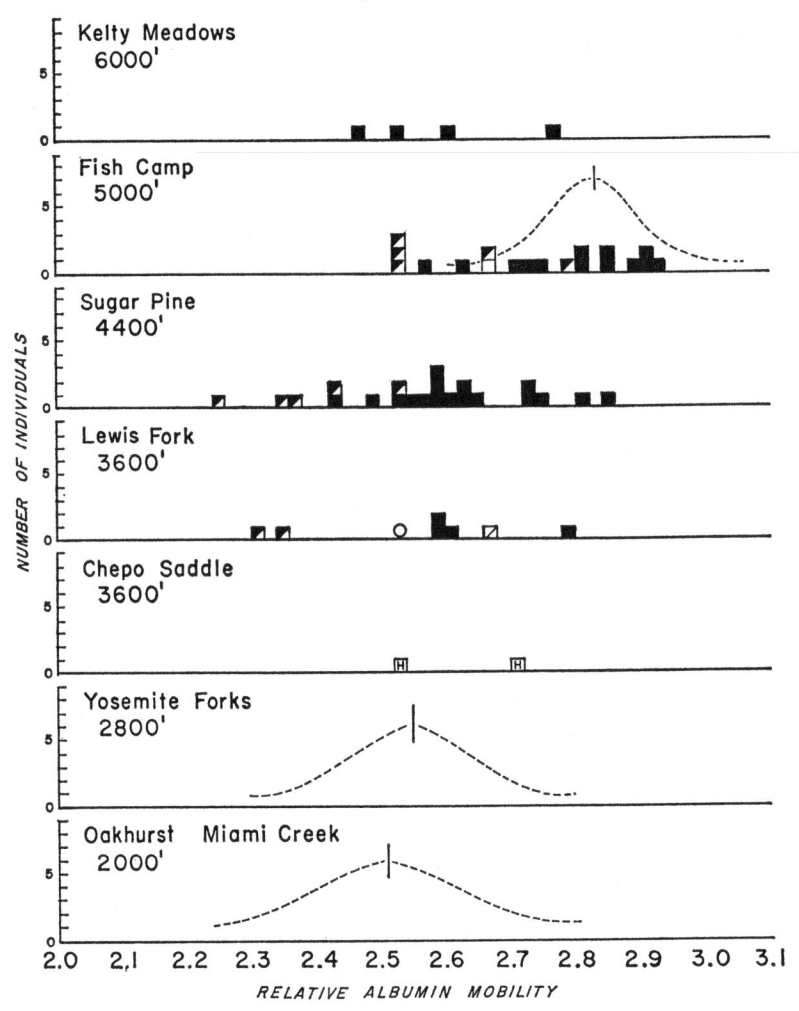

Fig. 21. Relative albumin mobilities for individuals of *Ensatina eschscholtzi* in populations from localities in Bass Lake region in Sierra Nevada. Horizontal axis: relative mobility of albumin peaks. Vertical axis: number of individuals from each locality. Solid squares represent primary albumin peaks of *platensis*; semi-solid squares represent secondary albumin peaks of *platensis*. Open circles represent primary albumin peaks of *xanthoptica*. No secondary peaks were found in *xanthoptice* from this region. Squares enclosing H represent albumin peaks for presumed F_1 hybrids. Dashed normal curve distribution lines represent predicted mobility distribution for *xanthoptica* populations at Yosemite Forks, Oakhurst, and Miami Creek, as based on study of population from Indian Creek, Calaveras County.

BASS LAKE REGION

The samples from the populations around Bass Lake are not as large as those from the Calaveras Big Trees Region, hence interpretation is more difficult (fig. 21). The trend, however, is roughly the same, with *platensis* tending to have faster mobility peaks than *xanthoptica*. *Platensis* from Sugar Pine, which is closer to the hybrid zone than Fish Camp, exhibits greater variation and slower mobility peaks than *platensis* at Fish Camp. However, the few data from Kelty Meadows indicate that this population may actually have slower albumin mobility than the population at Fish Camp or at Arnold. The populations at Fish Camp and at Arnold are roughly equivalent. The few individuals taken from the hybrid zones at Lewis Fork Creek and Chepo Saddle exhibit the expected high variability in mobility peaks, as well as peaks intermediate between *platensis* at Fish Camp or Arnold and *xanthoptica* at Indian Creek. The populations at Arnold and Indian Creek are used as representative for their subspecies.

It is interesting to note that none of the individuals at Kelty Meadows or Dorrington has secondary albumin peaks. Both of these localities seem to be the greatest distance from *xanthoptica* populations of the localities studied.

SAN GORGONIO REGION

Eschscholtzi from Sawmill Canyon and Mill Creek have two distinct peaks. The single specimen from Crystal Creek has a single albumin peak, intermediate between the two *eschscholtzi* peaks (fig. 22).

PALOMAR MOUNTAIN REGION

The sizeable sample from the locality adjacent to Palomar Observatory have albumin peaks which are also intermediate between two peaks possessed by *eschscholtzi* from San Gorgonio region. However, the *eschscholtzi* from Dyche and Will Valley possess albumin peaks at approximately the same mobility as *klauberi*. The one hybrid collected at Will Valley has three albumin peaks; two at the *eschscholtzi* positions and one at the *klauberi* position, as might be expected in an "ideal" intermediate. The backcross in Cedar Creek had only one peak at the faster mobility for *eschscholtzi* (fig. 22).

CONCLUSIONS AND SUMMARY

The trends shown thus far are interesting but inconclusive, and unfortunately, larger samples are needed for a satisfactory interpretation of the data. When comparing the major samples (fig. 23) some possible trends can be speculated upon. Generally, the blotched forms seems to have albumins which are faster than those of the unblotched ones. The trend from north to south indicates that there are slower albumins in the southern populations. Additional sampling may support the idea that *klauberi* has a single slow albumin peak, intermediate between two *eschscholtzi* peaks.

The significance of possessing slower albumin is not clearly understood. King and Jukes (1969) argue that most mutations resulting in amino acid substitutions in proteins are selectively neutral.[9] However, to pass off variations in *Ensatina*

---

[9] Many examples of animals to support the ideas of King and Jukes are drawn from domesticated forms. It is difficult and often dangerous to base concepts concerning *natural* selection on domesticated forms undergoing *artificial* selection. It is not difficult to see a rapid accumulation of so-called "neutral mutations" in laboratory rats or guinea pigs without apparent ill effects. In natural populations living and reproducing in their natural habitat, heavy losses of young and even a slightly lowered reproductivity of adults (due to a small genetic load) relative to those not possessing these mutations, would result in a shift in the gene frequency caused by natural selection. These processes often do not occur in laboratory or domestic forms, because of the highly modified and artificial environment in which these forms survive and reproduce.

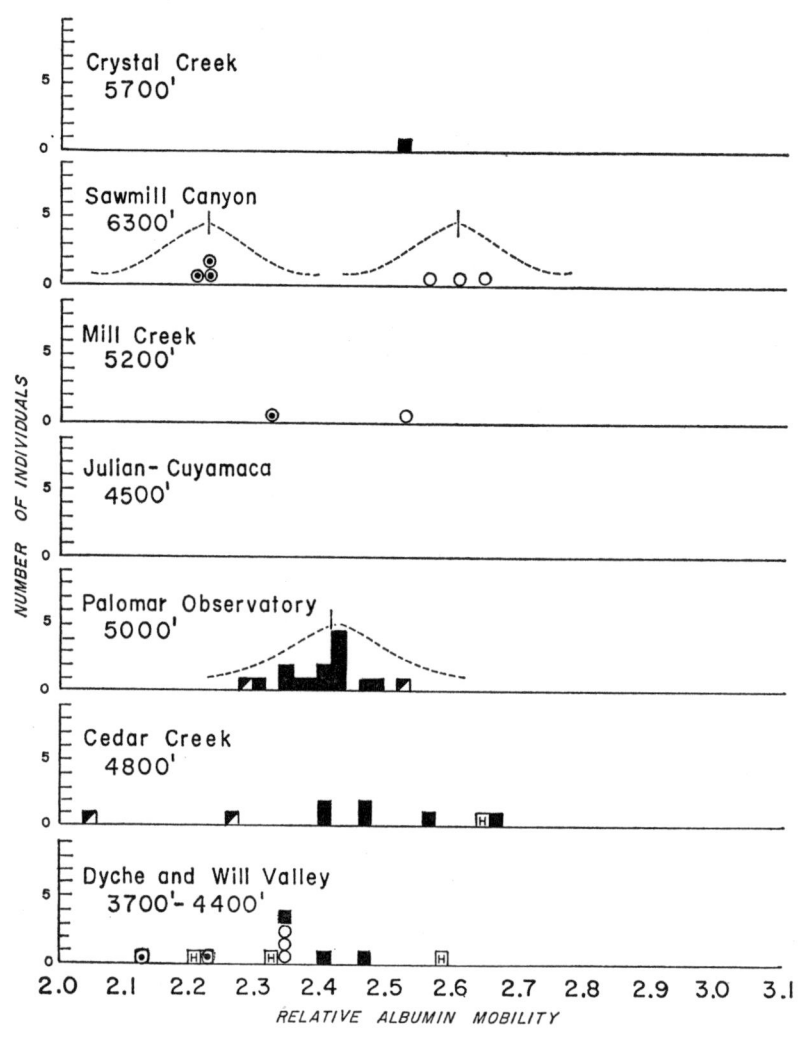

Fig. 22. Relative albumin mobilities for individuals of *Ensatina eschscholtzi* in populations from localities in Southern California. Horizontal axis: relative mobility of albumin peaks. Vertical axis: number of individuals for each locality. Solid squares represent primary albumin peaks for blotched individuals; semi-solid squares represent secondary albumin peaks for blotched individuals. Open circles represent primary albumin peaks for *eschscholtzi* individuals. Circles enclosing dots represent secondary albumin peaks for *eschscholtzi* individuals. Hybrid albumin peaks are squares enclosing an H. Dashed normal distribution curve lines represent possible albumin mobilities for selected blotched and unblotched populations.

albumins as neutral mutations does not seem warranted because of the apparent close correlations among albumin mobilities, morphological characteristics, and ecological conditions of the various subspecies.

It is clear that there are distinct differences between *picta* and *klauberi*. The other subspecies fall somewhere in between. The microheterogeneity existing between individuals within different populations might have been attributed to experimental error. However, when the entire picture of the north-to-south trend

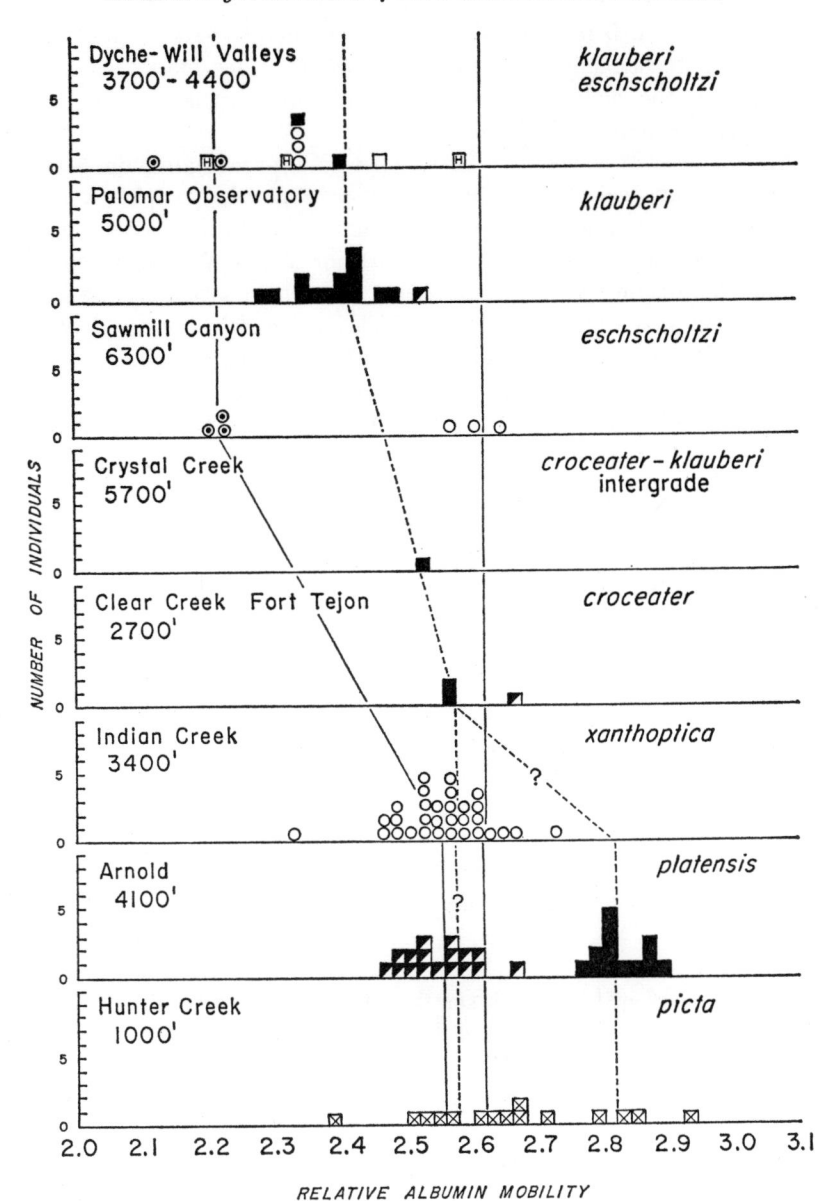

Fig. 23. Relative albumin mobilities for individuals of selected populations from the seven subspecies of *Ensatina eschscholtzi*. Horizontal axis: relative mobility of albumin peaks. Vertical axis: number of individuals from each locality. Solid squares represent primary albumin peaks for blotched individuals; semi-solid squares represent secondary albumin peaks for blotched individuals. Squares marked with an X represent individuals of the subspecies *picta*. Squares marked with an H represent hybrids. Open circles represent primary albumin peaks for unblotched individuals; circles enclosing dots represent secondary peaks for unblotched individuals. Dashed lines connecting blotched populations represent possible evolutionary change in mobility of primary albumin peaks. Solid lines connecting unblotched populations show possible evolutionary bifurcation in mobility of albumin peaks.

was evident, the 2 to 5 per cent differences among the various peaks indicated true changes in the chemistry of the albumins. It seems most likely that these changes were in the molecular size of the albumin, perhaps a polymerization process leading to increasing size.

This high degree of variability in number of separate albumin peaks found throughout the subspecies of *Ensatina* is very unusual. No other vertebrate is known to show such a high degree of albumin variability according to Lush (1966), Petrakis (personal communication), or Allen Wilson (personal communication). Theoretically, the genetic basis for such variation may be (1) partial gene duplication at a single gene locus which may lead in increased polypeptide length (2) multiple alleles for a given locus but present only in the usual pairs on the chromosomal homologues, (3) multiple factor effect of genes at different loci, and (4) modifying genes which are influenced by climatic conditions. Perhaps a combination of two or more above could give rise to the albumin phenotypes in *Ensatina* albumins.

Two variant forms of albumins, determined by co-dominant alleles, have been found in Shetland ponies and horses by Storment and Suzuki, and in Brown Leghorns by Mcindoe (after Lush, 1966). At the most three variant forms of albumins in Zebu cattle have been described by Ashton and Lampkin (after Lush, 1966).

It is difficult to explain the nature of *Ensatina* albumin peaks solely on the concept of gene duplication or multiple alleles involving a single gene locus (Petrakis and Brown, 1970). A few individuals show three peaks or even a single broad peak suggesting multiple factor effects. It is proposed here that the genetic basis for the high degree of variation in albumin peaks is a combination of several genetic mechanisms.

Thus the gradual increase in albumin size as seen in the slower peaks of the southern populations of *Ensatina* may be due to polymerization and/or increased polypeptide length of the albumins. In addition, fewer blood serum protein peaks in these southern populations may be a result of genetic drift. Southern California populations often seem to be both small and isolated and would satisfy requirements for the loss of certain alleles due to random fluctuations in the relative gene frequencies as set forth by Mayr (1963). If the populations are in fact large but simply difficult to collect, then genetic drift probably does not occur. Selective neutrality does not seem to be a logical base for genetic drift because of the possible pleiotropic effects of the so-called "neutral mutations" on the integrative functions of the genome.

Apparently the only correlation evident is with the snout-vent length of the subspecies. However, there may be a correlation between the relative albumin mobility and a factor of the habitat, perhaps involving temperature and available moisture. *Xanthoptica* may be subjected to generally higher temperatures than *platensis*, but has sufficient moisture available throughout the year. *Eschscholtzi*, however, may undergo stresses involving both warmer temperatures and desiccation—more so than *xanthoptica* or *klauberi*. In addition, *klauberi* may be subjected to somewhat warmer temperatures and less moisture than *platensis*. Detailed field studies are definitely needed to demonstrate a possible correlation, or lack of same, between environmental factors and relative albumin mobility. These studies should be coupled with an analysis of the physiological functions of blood serum albumin. Selective neutrality of these albumins may be the case, but it would be very difficult indeed to support such a concept with convincing data.

DISCUSSION

Mayr (1963), in his review of modern evolutionary findings, showed that geographic variations between populations (1) have a genetic basis, (2) are therefore a result of accumulations of micromutations, and (3) are ecologically adaptive. He also indicated that some phenotypic variations are due to environmental variation and may have the same genetic basis. Mayr has clearly pointed out the integrative nature of the entire genetic complex of the individual (genome), and because of the intricate web of interactions between genes, a single minor mutation may have many effects and thus would fit favorably into the balanced genome if these effects had a positive selective value. Thus in a continually changing environment there would be a "continuous adjustment of an integrated gene complex" by a given population.

Because most species show a greater or lesser degree of geographic variation, it follows that in these species there are a complex of genetic changes based on slow accumulations of micromutations. With sufficient genetic changes, reproductive isloating barriers can evolve between closely related populations, reducing or eliminating crosses between them.

It is proposed here that *Ensatina* provides a particularly illustrative example of speciation via slow accumulation of micromutations, as is demonstrated by the existence of partial reproductive isolation between populations of some subspecies.

Stebbins' (1957) suggestion that the terminal southernmost subspecies *eschscholtzi* and *klauberi* may coexist without interbreeding has been shown to be partially correct. In Cedar Creek and near Dyche Valley, Palomar Mountain Region, some degree of sympatry (cohabitation) has been observed among individuals which are typical for the blotched and unblotched forms (fig. 15). The low frequency of hybridization, the strong bimodality in color patterns, and differences in blood albumins all indicate a strong filtering of genes between blotched and unblotched populations. The fact that blotched and unblotched populations have been found to meet in several places, both in the Sierra Nevada and in Southern California, and that they show the same pattern of phenotypic discontinuity, supports the idea of a north-to-south genetic divergence via accumulation of micromutations leading to reproductive isolation. This then supports Stebbins's basic concept of the *Ensatina* Rassenkreis and the north-to-south genetic divergence. In fact, the very presence of the rare hybrids, and the absence of evidence for genetic swamping in most localities, where blotched and unblotched forms meet, provides positive supportive evidence.

These data also support the idea that introgressive hybridization between blotched and unblotched populations has increased variability in the parental forms. The low frequency of hybrids and the strong discontinuity in some phenotypic characters are an indication that this introgression has not been a self-accelerating process leading to gene swamping of the two parental forms.

G. L. Stebbins (1966) stated that "the significance of hybridization in evolution can be summarized by saying that it may provide a rapid increase in the size of the gene pool, from which natural selection for adaptation to a new habitat might quickly sort out entirely new adaptative gene complexes." Ehrlich and Holm (1963) noted that "variability of the parental types will be increased in the direction of the hybridizing entity, and the species or subspecies may be able to increase its range and move into habitats previously unoccupied."

However, Mayr (1963) indicated that the "total weight of available evidence contradicts the assumption that hybridization plays a major evolutionary role among higher animals." To what extent the increased variability in *platensis* has led, or is now leading, to more favorable adaptive gene complexes is not known. Perhaps introgression from the more arid-dwelling *xanthoptica* into the more montane-dwelling *platensis* enabled the blotched form *platensis* to move into lower and more southerly localities where *xanthoptica* does not occur. If so, this would be support for Stebbins' (1966) belief that "hybridization has played a larger role in animal evolution than many zoologists think it has." Some evidence for this may be seen when comparing the albumin peaks of *croceater*, *klauberi* and the *secondary* peaks of *platensis*. The secondary albumin peaks of *platensis* resemble the primary peaks of *xanthoptica*. The slower albumin peaks may be a better adaptation to drier and warmer conditions as *eschscholtzi* and *klauberi* both have slower peaks than the other races. One should not exclude the possibility that *croceater* and *klauberi* populations evolved from *platensis*-like forms with genetic introgression from *xanthoptica*. This could account for the similarity in the above-mentioned albumin peaks.

Nagle and Mettler (1969) have given evidence to support the idea that introgression via hybridization can lead to increased adaptive fitness in parental populations. It was found that the interspecific populations (hybrids) which were polymorphic with respect to specific inversions, were adaptively inferior to intraspecific polymorphic populations of the parental types. That is to say the backcrosses, resulting from hybrids interbreeding with parental types, were better buffered developmentally than the hybrids. It was concluded that introgression can lead to enhancement of the fitness of the parental populations. This may be the case with *Ensatina* as well.

The selective advantage of the color patterns in the various populations of *Ensatina* is not clear. To the human eye, these salamanders are highly cryptic in their natural habitat. For example, *picta* is protectively colored very well in its natural redwood habitat near Crescent City, Del Norte County, California. When highly blotched individuals of the subspecies *klauberi* are placed on the low contrast background in the redwood habitat of *picta*, these *klauberi* are more clearly visible even though the individuals used in this study are approximately the same size as the selected *picta* individuals. *Klauberi* is very difficult to see on the high contrast background of Incense Cedar and Black Oak of Palomar Mountain Region, the habitat for this blotched form.

Platensis is very difficult to see on all backgrounds, but particularly so in its natural habitat. The Sierran *xanthoptica* however, is not only visible, but obvious on all backgrounds, including the habitat in which it is found. For these reasons I propose here that all subspecies of *Ensatina eschscholtzi* have adapted cryptically to the background coloration of their respective habitats except the race *xanthoptica* in the Sierra Nevada. Since *xanthoptica* is so overtly obvious on all backgrounds, being a distinct bright orange-red color, it seems reasonable that this race has evolved warning coloration, perhaps a mimicry of *Taricha*, which live in the same general areas. Stebbins (personal communication) feels that the subspecies *eschscholtzi* is as conspicuous as Sierran *xanthoptica*, and this may be due to a trogloditic life resulting in a loss of melanophores.

The apparent adaptive pigmentation of *Ensatina* is fairly clear in terms of pattern but much less so in terms of color. The cryptic value of the color is questionable as it is not certain which predators now, or in the past, have affected *Ensatina* populations. But the facts remain: (1) to the human observer, individuals of each subspecies match most closely, both in pattern and in color, the background of the habitat in which they are found, and (2) when individuals are kept in captivity, mold which has the color of the salamander will grow on the paper towels in that particular jar.[10] These data support strongly the belief that, except for the Sierran *xanthoptica*, all subspecies are concealingly colored against the attacks of predators.

There are other possible explanations for the pigmentation in *Ensatina*. It is possible that the coloration is used in sexual recognition and courtship. However, no significant pigmentation differences are found between the sexes of a given population. Also, pigmentation may be merely a phenotypic byproduct of some pleiotropic effect. If this is true, then the close match of the pigmentation to the background is a remarkable coincidence. Finally, no evidence can be found to support the idea that thse color patterns merely demonstrate balanced polymorphism.

SUMMARY

Ensatina eschscholtzi is a polytypic species that is conveniently divided into seven subspecies. These subspecies are: *picta, oregonensis, xanthoptica,* and *eschscholtzi*, distributed along the coastal mountains, and *platensis, xanthoptica, croceater,* and *klauberi*, found in the interior mountains of California. The populations of *E. eschscholtzi* are roughly distributed in a circle forming a Rassenkreis. Analysis of color patterns and blood serum proteins indicate that there seems to be a north-to-south gradient in genetic divergence between the blotched and unblotched forms. In the mountins of northern California there is a smooth broad zone of intergradation between *oregonensis* and *platensis*. In the central Sierra Nevada near Avery, Jawbone Ridge and Bass Lake, there is a narrow zone of hybridization, and there is a fairly sharp discontinuity in color patterns between adjacent populations of *xanthoptica* and *platensis*. Hybrids are found in this

---

[10] It is interesting to note the color of the molds, which grow on paper towels, apparently brought in on the surface or in the gut of salamanders. In the case of the unblotched coastal *xanthoptica*, the molds are of one color almost matching the color of the dorsal surface of these individuals. For blotched forms such as *klauberi*, the molds are of two colors, one matching the color of the blotches and the other a dark color, almost black!

narrow zone but are very uncommon. This phenotypic discontinuity is generally associated with an abrupt change in the habitat such as vegetation, depth of leaf litter, rainfall, and temperature.

In southern California, there is an even greater distinction between the blotched forms (*croceater* and *klauberi*) and the unblotched *eschscholtzi*. Furthermore, some evidence exists for a narrow zone of sympatry with little evidence of introgression. Apparent hybrids and hybrid backcrosses between *eschscholtzi* and *klauberi* (3.5 percent) are fewer in number than those found between *xanthoptica* and *platensis* populations (8 percent). There is also a marked distinction in habitats of *klauberi* and *eschscholtzi*.

Electrophoretic analysis of blood serum proteins have also demonstrated differences among the various subspecies. In general there seems to be marked differences between *xanthoptica* and *platensis* in the position of the albumin peak. However, in areas of hybridization, some *platensis* show evidence of *xanthoptica* peaks. Differences in relative albumin peak mobilities between *klauberi* and *eschscholtzi* is not so clear. The subspecies *picta*, located in northwestern California and southeastern Oregon, is believed by Stebbins (1949) to be close to if not actually the ancestral form from which all other *Ensatina* populations were derived. Color patterns support this belief, as *picta* seems to have all necessary elements on which natural selection could act and produce other subspecies. This is also true for the blood serum proteins. *Picta* is highly variable in the albumin peaks. Although a few *klauberi* demonstrate a shift of the albumin to the right of those of *picta* (smaller faster moving molecules), *klauberi* more often has an albumin peak resembling *eschscholtzi*, which is shifted to the left side of the *picta* albumins (larger slower-moving molecules).

Color photographs of some of the subspecies seem to indicate that the subtle as well as the overt differences in color patterns found among the subspecies have a high cryptic value. The significance of the differences in the ventral colorations are not yet understood. It is possible that the bright coloration of Sierran *xanthoptica* acts as a warning sign to predators, as it is highly conspicuous on all backgrounds.

LITERATURE CITED

BROWN, C. W., and R. C. STEBBINS
    1964. "Evidence for hybridization between the blotched and unblotched subspecies of the salamander *Ensatina eschscholtzi*." *Evolution* 18:706–707.

DAVIS, B. J.
    1964. "Disc electrophoresis, II, method and application to human serum proteins." *Ann. New York Acad. Sci.* 121: 404–427.

DESSAUER, H. C., W. FOX, and F. H. POUGH
    1962. "Starch-gel electrophoresis of transferrins, esterases, and other plasma proteins of hybrids between two subspecies of whiptail lizard (genus *Cnemidophorus*)." *Copeia*, no. 4: 767–774.

DODSON, E. O.
    1952. *A Texbook of Evolution*. Philadelphia: Sanders.

DUNN, E. R.
    1929. "A new salamander from southern California." *Proc. U.S. Nat. Mus.* 74(25):1–3.

EHRLICH, P. R., and R. W. HOLM
    1963. *The Process of Evolution*. San Francisco: McGraw-Hill.

FINDLEY, J. S.
    1955. "Speciation of the Wandering Shrew." *Univ. Kan. Publ. Mus. Nat. Hist.* 9(1):1–68.

KING, J. L., and T. H. JUKES
    1969. Non-Darwinian evolution. *Science*, 164:788–798.

LUSH, I. E.
    1966. *The Biochemical Genetics of Vertebrates Except Man*. Amsterdam: North-Holland Publ. Co.

MAYR, ERNST
    1963. *Animal Species and Evolution*. Cambridge, Mass.: Harvard Univ. Press.

MUNSELL BOOK OF COLOR
    1943. Baltimore, Md.: Munsell Color Co.

NAGLE, J. J. and L. E. METLER
    1969. "Relative fitness of introgressed and parental populations of *Drosophila mojavensis* and *D. arizonensis*." *Evolution*, 23(4):519–524.

PETRAKIS, P. L.
    1969. "An inexpensive high-resolution densitometer for disc electrophoresis." *Anal. Biochem.* 28:416–427.

PETRAKIS, P. L., and C. W. BROWN
    1970. "A high order of heterogeneity in the serm albumin of *Ensatina eschscholtzi*, a Pacific Coast salamander." *Comp Biochem. Physiol.* 32:475–487.

RENSCH, BERNARD
    1929. *Das Prinzip Geographischer Rassenkreise und das Problem der Artbildung*. Berlin.
    1960. *Evolution Above the Species Level*. N.Y., Columbia University Press.

SALTHE, S. N.
    1969. "Geographic variation of the lactate dehydrogenases of *Rana pipiens* and *Rana palustris*." *Biochemical Genetics*, 2:271–303.

SIBLEY, C. G.
    1950. "Species formation in the Red-eyed Towhees of Mexico." *Univ. of Calif. Publ. Zool.* 50:109–194.

STEBBINS, G. L.
    1966. *Processes of Organic Evolution*. Englewood Cliffs, N.J.: Prentice-Hall.

STEBBINS, R. C.
    1949. *Speciation in salamanders of the plethodontid genus Ensatina*. Univ. Calif. Publ. Zool. 48(6):377–526.
    1954. *Natural history of the salamanders of the plethodontid genus Ensatina*. Univ. Calif. Publ. Zool. 54(2):47–124.
    1957. "Intraspecific sympatry in the lungless salamander *Ensatina eschscholtzi*." *Evolution*. 11(3):265–270.

ZWEIFEL, R. G.
    1962. "Analysis of hybridization between two subspecies of the desert whiptail lizard, *Cnemidophorus tigris. Copeia*, no. 4:749–766.

PLATES

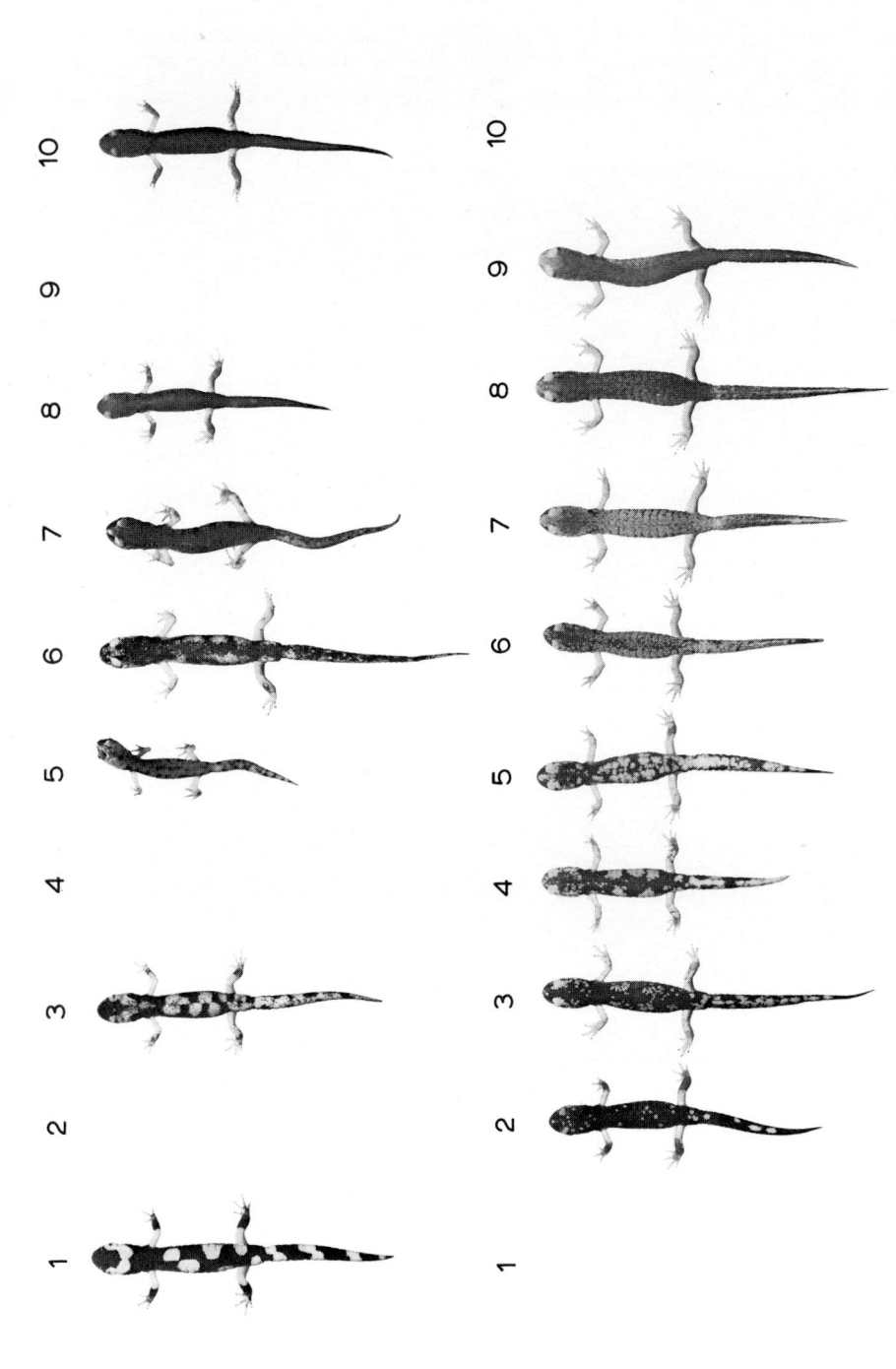

Variation in dorsal blotching in *Ensatina eschscholtzi*. Upper series: Range in degree of dorsal blotching observed in Southern California populations. Value of 1 = "pure" blotched *klauberi*. Value of 10 = "pure" unblotched *eschscholtzi*. Lower series: Range in degree of dorsal blotching observed in Sierra Nevada populations. Value of 2 = "pure" blotched *platensis*. Value of 10 = "pure" unblotched *xanthoptica*. Intermediate values of 5 and 6 represent presumed F_1 hybrid patterns. Values of 3 and 4 represent presumed hybrid × *klauberi* backcrosses. Values of 7 and 8 represent presumed hybrid × *eschscholtzi* backcrosses.

Ensatina eschscholtzi picta habitat. Prairie Creek Redwoods State Park, Del Norte County, California.

Ensatina eschscholtzi platensis habitat. Fish Camp, Bass Lake region, Mariposa County, California.

Ensatina eschscholtzi xanthoptica habitat. Yosemite Forks, Bass Lake region, Madera County, California.

WITHDRAWN